CHAUCER STUDIES VI

SYNTAX AND STYLE IN CHAUCER'S POETRY

CHAUCER STUDIES

I
MUSIC IN THE AGE OF CHAUCER
Nigel Wilkins

II
CHAUCER'S LANGUAGE AND THE PHILOSOPHERS' TRADITION
J. D. Burnley

III
ESSAYS ON TROILUS AND CRISEYDE
Edited by Mary Salu

IV
CHAUCER SONGS
Nigel Wilkins

V
CHAUCER'S BOCCACCIO
Sources of Troilus *and the* Knight's *and* Franklin's Tales
Edited and translated by N. R. Havely

SYNTAX AND STYLE IN CHAUCER'S POETRY

G. H. ROSCOW

D. S. BREWER · ROWMAN & LITTLEFIELD

First published 1981 by D. S. Brewer
240 Hills Road, Cambridge
an imprint of Boydell & Brewer Ltd, PO Box 9,
Woodbridge, Suffolk IP12 3DF
and Rowman & Littlefield Inc, 81 Adams Drive,
Totowa, New Jersey N.J. 07512, USA

British Library Cataloguing in Publication Data

Roscow, Gregory
    Syntax and style in Chaucer's poetry.—(Chaucer studies; 6)
    1. Chaucer, Geoffrey—Criticism and interpretation
    I. Title. II. Series
    821'.1   ~~PR1924~~ PR 1948, R67
    ISBN 0-85991-080-6

    US ISBN 0-8476-7053-8

TO MY MOTHER AND FATHER

Photoset in Great Britain by
Rowland Phototypesetting Ltd, Bury St Edmunds, Suffolk
and printed by St Edmundsbury Press
Bury St Edmunds, Suffolk

Contents

PREFACE

This book is intended as a contribution to the study of Chaucer's syntax and style. It is by no means a comprehensive survey, for little is said directly about the functions of the parts of speech, and even within the areas of usage chosen for discussion the treatment is necessarily selective. Nevertheless, it is hoped that the selection will be found useful in its attention to structural and idiomatic features of Chaucer's syntax that have received little comment in the past or have been examined from a different point of view. The more particular aims of the book are explained in the introductory chapter.

Quotations from Chaucer are taken from *The Works of Geoffrey Chaucer*, edited by F. N. Robinson, second edition (Cambridge, Mass., 1957), though here and elsewhere I have occasionally altered the punctuation in order to clarify points of construction. Abbreviated titles of Chaucer's poems are listed on p. ix, and those of other texts are explained in the Bibliography. References to numbered poems in an anthology specify the number of the poem before the line-reference (e.g. *HarlLyr* 32.1), and to prose the number of the page (e.g. *MandTravels* 8/20). References to secondary material are to the author's name and, where necessary, the year of publication; details will be found in the Bibliography.

I am grateful to Mr A. C. Spearing, the late Professor J. A. W. Bennett, Dr D. S. Brewer, Dr Jill Mann, and Professor J. A. Burrow for reading and commenting on parts of this book in an earlier form, and to Dr Brewer also for undertaking to publish it. To Mr Spearing I owe a special debt, both for his generous help and encouragement when I was a research student at Cambridge, and for the stimulating example of his writings on medieval poetry. Needless to say, the responsibility for any inaccuracy is entirely my own.

Keele, Staffordshire,
August 1981

vii

ABBREVIATIONS

Abbreviated Titles of Chaucer's Poems

ABC	*An ABC*
Anel	*Anelida and Arcite*
BD	*The Book of the Duchess*
Buk	*Lenvoy de Chaucer a Bukton*
ClT	*The Clerk's Tale*
CYProl	*The Canon's Yeoman's Prologue*
CYT	*The Canon's Yeoman's Tale*
FormAge	*The Former Age*
Fort	*Fortune*
FranklT	*The Franklin's Tale*
FrT	*The Friar's Tale*
GenProl	*The General Prologue*
Gent	*Gentilesse*
HF	*The House of Fame*
KnT	*The Knight's Tale*
Lady	*A Complaint to his Lady*
LGW	*The Legend of Good Women*
MancT	*The Manciple's Tale*
Mars	*The Complaint of Mars*
MerchT	*The Merchant's Tale*
MillT	*The Miller's Tale*
MkT	*The Monk's Tale*
MLT	*The Man of Law's Tale*
NPT	*The Nun's Priest's Tale*
PardProl	*The Pardoner's Prologue*
PardT	*The Pardoner's Tale*
PF	*The Parliament of Fowls*
PhysT	*The Physicians's Tale*
Pity	*The Complaint unto Pity*
PrT	*The Prioress's Tale*
Rom	*The Romaunt of the Rose*
RvT	*The Reeve's Tale*
Scog	*Lenvoy de Chaucer a Scogan*
SecNT	*The Second Nun's Tale*
ShipT	*The Shipman's Tale*
SqT	*The Squire's Tale*
SumT	*The Summoner's Tale*
Thop	*Sir Thopas*
Tr	*Troilus and Criseyde*
Ven	*The Complaint of Venus*
WBProl	*The Wife of Bath's Prologue*
WBT	*The Wife of Bath's Tale*
WomNob	*Womanly Noblesse*

Other Abbreviations

BTSuppl	Supplement to *An Anglo-Saxon Dictionary*, edited by T. Northcote Toller (Oxford, 1921)
EETS, ES	Early English Text Society (Original Series), Extra Series
Glossary	*A Chaucer Glossary*, compiled by Norman Davis, Douglas Gray, Patricia Ingham, and Anne Wallace-Hadrill (Oxford, 1979)
ME.	Middle English
MED	*Middle English Dictionary*, edited by Hans Kurath and Sherman M. Kuhn (Ann Arbor, 1952–)
MnE.	Modern English
OE.	Old English
OED	*The Oxford English Dictionary*
OFr.	Old French
ON.	Old Norse
PMLA	*Publications of the Modern Language Association of America*
s.v.	*sub voce* 'under the word . . .' (in references to dictionaries)

CHAPTER I

Introduction

Probably the most familiar comment on the syntax of ME. poetry is that it tends to be somewhat loose and illogical compared with that of literary usage in later periods, and to bear a closer resemblance to the structure of the spoken language. Chaucer's syntax in particular has often been described as conversational in its tolerance for the kind of looseness to be seen in the following passage:

> And certes in the same book I rede,
> Right in the nexte chapitre after this—
> I gabbe nat, so have I joye or blis—
> Two men that wolde han passed over see,
> For certeyn cause, into a fer contree,
> If that the wynd ne hadde been contrarie,
> That made hem in a citee for to tarie
> That stood ful myrie upon an haven-syde;
> But on a day, agayn the even-tyde,
> The wynd gan chaunge, and blew right as hem leste.
>
> *(NPT* 3064-73)

The construction in lines 3067–71 is an incomplete form of recursiveness on the pattern of 'The cat that chased the rat that ate the corn . . .', which is abandoned in favour of a fresh start with the phrase 'But on a day'. At one time such lapses were attributed to the poet himself; according to Kenneth Sisam, 'Chaucer gets lost in the succession of subordinate clauses beginning with *that*, and there is no formal predicate to *two men*' (p. 42). The tendency of more recent critical opinion, however, may be suggested by substituting Chauntecleer for Chaucer in this quotation; it is the speaker who gets lost in the tangle of details, not the poet, who by means of anacoluthon subtly deflates Chauntecleer's fussy prolixity. In view of the context, and of the fact that this inconsequential construction could easily have been avoided by writing 'That two men wolde' in line 3067, it would seem reasonable to consider

I

it a deliberate slip used to mirror the speaker's wayward train of thought. Chauntecleer may not 'gabbe', but he certainly gabbles.

Modern criticism has largely shifted the responsibility for loose syntax from the poet to his characters. What were once regarded as pardonable lapses due to carelessness or to the unsettled state of the language have instead been described by Margaret Schlauch as 'fitting lapses' by which 'Chaucer shows an ear attuned to people's idioms according to character, circumstance, and social level' (p. 1116). While this represents an advance in critical attention to Chaucer's style, the characterisation of loose syntax as colloquial which it promotes must be treated with caution. The claim that 'the more colloquial passages show character- istics of informal English which are recognizable as deviations from the contrasting formal usages of both Chaucer's age and ours' (p. 1104) is liable to give a misleading impression, since the same features are to be found in formal contexts in Chaucer's poetry and so cannot be colloquial in the strict sense of the term. The fact that Miss Schlauch often has recourse to a useful distinction between literary and colloquial functions of loose syntax acknowledges that the various forms of pleonasm, ellip- sis, and anacoluthon under consideration are for the most part stylisti- cally neutral, and depend for their effect on the context of situation and the diction of the sentences in which they are used. Moreover, while it is obviously true that, so far as linguistic form is concerned, Chaucer's syntax 'reveals several patterns which we can recognize by their kinship with our own habits' (p. 1112), we cannot automatically assign similar stylistic functions to these patterns on the strength of their structural resemblance to those in present-day English. To do so would lead us to conclude that Lucresse is lapsing into sub-standard usage when she says 'I wol not have noo forgyft for nothing' (*LGW* 1853), as if she were the heroine of *West Side Story*. The fate of multiple negation in English is a convenient reminder that the relationship between linguistic form and stylistic function can vary quite considerably from one period to another, and that we can as easily misread a passage of earlier literature by giving modern values to its syntax as by giving modern meanings to its voca- bulary.

At this point it may be helpful to consider two representative instances of what Miss Schlauch regards as colloquial usage. The first occurs in the carpenter's brief reflection on worldly instability in *The Miller's Tale*:

> This world is now ful tikel, sikerly.
> I saugh to-day a cors yborn to chirche
> *That* now, on Monday last, I saugh *hym* wirche.   (3428–30)

Miss Schlauch detects a 'delightfully appropriate colloquialism' in the second sentence:

> Here the grammatical dislocation accords with the illogicality of undisciplined speech. Who can parse the relative pronoun *that*; and who can envisage the antecedent corpse at work in the fields on Monday last? (p. 1114)

2

The fact that the carpenter uses a construction which, in its positive form, is as rare in Chaucer's poetry as the word *tikel* may well suggest that it is intended as a device of characterisation, but does it tell us that he is illogical and undisciplined in his speech? Miss Schlauch's claim that the reinforced relative form *that . . . hym* effects a significant dislocation is in fact somewhat misleading, since it is clear from her questions that, the point at issue being one of logic rather than grammar, the expression of the personal pronoun *hym* is immaterial. What is odd from a logical point of view is the absence of a term like 'man' to supply a link between the relative and its antecedent ('the corpse *of a man* whom I saw'); but this has nothing to do with the form of the relative clause, and in any case there is no reason to suppose that Chaucer and his contemporaries would have analysed the sentence in this way. On the contrary, it can be argued that the carpenter's characteristically homely observation obeys a logic of its own that justifies, indeed requires, the use of a reinforced relative clause. The construction lends an apt concreteness to the expression of mutability by formally acknowledging the two different states in which the object of attention is perceived: as a corpse (*that*) and as the man he once was (*hym*). Chaucer exploits the flexible resources of his language in order to produce an economical form of statement that is appropriate not because it now seems to us undisciplined, but because it is in accord with the blunt, practical manner of a self-confessed 'lewed man' who views life in concrete terms and has no use for the abstract world of learning—an attitude that proves to be his undoing. Part of the point of the story is lost if we are encouraged to think of him as a silly old man who cannot construct a decent sentence; he is rather a man who prides himself on seeing life steadily, and sees it piecemeal. His use of the reinforced relative clause thus serves a more particular purpose than is allowed for by treating it as an illogical colloquialism.

The second example of loose structure quoted by Miss Schlauch is when 'the Apothecary in the *Pardoner's Tale* introduces a similar loose clause in his verbose praise of the poison he is about to sell' (p. 1114):

> And thou shalt have
> A thyng that, also God my soule save,
> In al this world there is no creature,
> That eten or dronken hath of this confiture
> Noght but the montance of a corn of whete,
> *That he* ne shal his lif anon forlete. (859–64)

What might seem at first a fairly lax sentence in which the clauses are loosely strung together with *that*s is in fact a sustained period of some force. There is an orderly progression of ideas, with *that* appearing first as a consecutive conjunction equivalent to 'such that' (this is the key to the structure of the sentence), then as a relative pronoun to introduce a clause describing the prospective action, and finally, in the line Miss Schlauch considers to be loose, as a relative pronoun reinforced by *he* to introduce a clause describing the result of the action: that is, 'You shall have such a thing that there is nobody who has tasted it who will not die

3

at once'. Far from being an idiosyncrasy, the use of the reinforced relative clause in the last line is normal ME. practice in negative sentences of this kind (see p. 106 below), and it is a construction that is particularly adapted to the purpose of emphatic expression by virtue of its similarity to the structure of consecutive clauses. The forceful effect of this sentence is augmented by the use of an inverted consecutive construction (see p. 137) to conclude the speech:

> Ye, sterve he shal, and that in lasse while
> Than thou wolt goon a paas nat but a mile,
> This poysoun is so strong and violent. (865–7)

[handwritten marginalia: "still colloquial"]

In a later comment Miss Schlauch claims that 'the basically dislocated sentence put into the mouth of the solemn Apothecary' is 'strikingly appropriate to the speaker' (p. 1116). But even if we overlook the fact that his syntax is altogether normal, it is surely irrelevant to Chaucer's purpose to portray the character of this functional figure. Throughout the passage our attention is directed not to the person of the apothecary, who has been introduced into the narrative without a word of description, but to the nature of the poison which he sells to one of the revellers. He emerges suddenly and briefly from the shadows of this dark tale in order to give expression to the horrifying power coveted by the reveller, a power that is forcibly suggested by the emphatic structure of his sentences.

[handwritten marginalia: "Indeed because of his speech"]

The syntax in these lines from *The Pardoner's Tale* may be seen to serve a non-dramatic, mimetic function, which Donald Davie in his discussion of the varieties of poetic syntax defines as being 'to please us by the fidelity with which it follows a form of action, a movement not through any mind, but in the world at large' (p. 79). That this function has received comparatively little attention in the study of medieval poetry no doubt results in part from the characterisation of ME. syntax as colloquial and therefore dramatically significant. Greater attention deserves to be given to syntactical means of securing mimetic effects, which range from simple forms of enactment, such as the use of ellipsis and co-ordination to convey an impression of rapid movement, to the representation of plots in miniature, as in the following lines from the Zenobia episode in *The Monk's Tale*:

> Allas, Fortune! *she* that whilom was
> Dredeful to kynges and to emperoures,
> Now gaureth al the peple on *hire*, allas! (2367–9)

There is little to be gained from attributing this abrupt shift in construction, a variety of *nominativus pendens* (see p. 76), to the Monk himself as a device of characterisation; it has instead a mimetic function in enacting the heroine's sudden reversal of fortune. A form of action is vividly traced as the sentence presses forward past the ominous contrast between *whilom* and *now* to the verb *gaureth*, which by virtue of its

[handwritten marginalia: "True"]

position momentarily offers to complete the expected structure, and then provides the verb with a new subject altogether, leaving Zenobia as the literal and grammatical object of the people's curiosity. The expression of reversal, affectingly framed by the repetition of *allas*, is all the more poignant in view of previous emphasis on the heroine's physical strength and sturdy independence. Effects of this kind are not accounted for by Miss Schlauch's general comment that 'artful anacoluthon uses such reorientations of syntax deliberately, in the midst of elaborate and well-composed sentences, in order to indicate confused sentiments or frustration' (p. 1115). *Exactly right!*

The characterisation of loose syntax as colloquial tends to restrict us to a rather narrow range of its literary functions in medieval poetry. We are encouraged to give particular attention to passages of dialogue, where it is reasonable to expect features of colloquial usage to occur most prominently, and to account for such features in terms of their dramatic propriety as exponents of character. While this approach has undoubtedly sharpened our response to syntactical mannerisms in the speech of such chatty individuals as the Wife of Bath, it leaves us with little to say about the use of the same constructions by more formal speakers and by the poet himself in narrative. Although at the end of her article Miss Schlauch observes that 'Chaucer himself inserts loose colloquial structures into many expository passages', her conclusion is merely that they 'contribute to the sense of happy ease and flowingness which were characteristic of the poetry in all its periods, from the early *Book of the Duchess* to the maturest of the *Canterbury Tales*' (p. 1116). Chaucer is thus treated in the main as a dramatic rather than a narrative poet. But even within the sphere of dialogue the emphasis on the colloquial nature of loose syntax can often imply a degree of informality that is not noticed by other speakers in the text, and it also frequently issues in a pyschological interpretation that equates loose constructions with disordered thoughts. In both cases the effect of appealing to a sense of 'kinship with our own habits', however attractive this may seem in making the language more familiar, is to impose on medieval texts a conception of correct grammar that is largely the product of eighteenth-century rationalism. There is no more reason to regard the ME. equivalent of 'That man, I saw him yesterday' as colloquial than there is its equivalent in modern French, which tolerates the construction at various levels of style. There is even less reason to assume that quite normal ME. contructions that now seem loose to us were formerly indicative of illogical and undisciplined modes of thought.

Norman Blake in a recent general study of the language of Old and Middle English literature has also questioned the familiar characterisation of loose syntax, though not in the belief that it inhibits sytlistic analysis; on the contrary, he argues that 'the average reader and writer did not have any real sense of acceptable syntax', and therefore 'syntax could not be manipulated so easily for stylistic or other ends' (p. 153). Fortunately, this challenge to the practice of close reading, in reviving an older view that Early English 'wanteth grammar', is not altogether convincing. As an example of the 'lack of regulation in the medieval language as a whole'—an observation intended to apply to seven

5

centuries of English writing—we are offered the following comments on the use of tenses in a familiar passage of late ME. poetry:

> When translation is not involved, the verb forms are often simpler and perhaps even less logical in their arrangement. If for example we look at the opening of *Sir Gawain and the Green Knight*, the siege of Troy is introduced in the first line in the perfect tense: *watʒ sesed*. Then the author uses the preterite (*wroʒt*) to describe the man who committed treason, though the perfect again (*watʒ tried*) for his trial. Afterwards he subjected, in the preterite (*depreced*) kingdoms, though the other extensions of Trojan influence are mentioned in the present tense (*ricchis, biges* etc.). Although Brutus occupies England in the present tense, since his time many changes have taken place in the perfect (*hatʒ wont, hatʒ skyfted*). Modern English renderings of the poem usually rearrange these verb forms in a more coherent order, for it is difficult to see any rational progression of the tenses in the poem itself. There was a gradual extension of verb forms in Middle English, but a sifting out and ordering of their meaning came only later. Variety of form precedes variety of meaning. (p. 152)

Are we really to believe that the *Gawain*-poet chose his tenses at random? An author who was so muddled in his syntax as this analysis suggests would scarcely be able to express the simplest of notions, let alone the intricacies of courtly thought and behaviour. However, while a prescriptive grammarian might prefer *wroʒt* to be in the pluperfect, the sequence of tenses in the opening lines is normal enough, *watʒ tried* being of course a preterite passive form and not a perfect: 'After the siege *had ceased*, the man who *committed* treason *was tried* for his treachery'. The only difference from modern usage comes with the introduction of verbs in the historic present tense for the sake of vividness, a common device of later medieval narrative poetry that Professor Blake treats as a casual idiosyncrasy. Whatever the truth of the remark that 'variety of form precedes variety of meaning' may be as a principle of linguistic evolution, it is not illustrated by the passage chosen; nor is it generally applicable to the use of tenses elsewhere in ME. literature.

Other features of loose syntax such as faulty concord and ellipsis are mentioned more briefly, and Professor Blake concludes by indicating the kinds of stylistic effects which it was not possible for medieval writers to achieve. Something of his insistence on deficiencies and irregularities of Early English syntax may be explained by a concern that modern studies 'necessarily arrange the available material into general rules and trends, and so unwittingly create the impression that the language at the time was more regulated and systematic than it was' (p. 137). But a language that is not regulated by formal instruction in grammar is no less systematic than one that is. If general rules framed at the present day are misleading, it is because they neglect the finer points of earlier usage which only a close study can reveal; the short-comings of generalisation are not made good by banishing exceptions to the realm of unsystematic and therefore meaningless variation. In any case, Professor Blake's own generalisations are rather less satisfactory than the sort which he seems anxious to displace. There is little support in the literature for such sweeping claims as that 'in medieval English it was difficult to make up complex sentences with many subordinate clauses' (p. 144), which take us back to a time when Early English syntax was thought a primitive instrument of expression.

We have been considering two rather different approaches to loose syntax, one of them assuming a close correspondence between medieval and modern usage, and the other emphasising their remoteness. What these studies have in common is a tendency to regard loose constructions as illogical and undisciplined. Some of the problems arising from this characterisation might be avoided by describing general features of ME. syntax in terms that are less prejudicial to the analysis of stylistic effects. For example, it has been said with particular reference to vocabulary that 'fourteenth-century English falls naturally into . . . physical conceptions of events' (Spearing 1972, p. 47), and this observation can be seen to apply also to certain aspects of syntax. The element of concreteness in the syntax of earlier periods of English was given some attention in the last century by Leon Kellner, who mentions one construction in particular that suggests a 'physical conception of events':

> What was formerly called *prolepsis*, or redundant object, is simply an interesting remnant of the old concrete way of forming noun-clauses. We now say 'he saw that the work was good', the noun-clause being apprehended as abstract; but the biblical expression 'he saw the work that it was good', is psychologically the only correct one. (pp. 18–19)

A knowledge of this construction (see p. 81 below) helps to illuminate an interesting passage in *The House of Fame* in which the narrator describes an episode in the story of Aeneas portrayed on a wall in the temple of Venus:

> Ther saugh I graven eke withal,
> Venus, how *ye*, my lady dere,
> Wepynge with ful woful chere,
> *Prayen* Jupiter on hye
> To save and kepe that navye
> Of the Troian Eneas,
> Syth that he *hir* sone *was*.   (*HF* 212–18)

As the italicised forms indicate, the sentence appears to lurch somewhat disconcertingly from direct address in the present tense to narration in the preterite; and we might wish to account for the shift in construction as evidence of the narrator's uncertain handling of his material, or simply as an instance of undisciplined ME. usage. Removal of the editorial comma after *withal*, however, reveals a concrete noun clause, which is more normal Chaucerian syntax than the use of a vocative in this position. By means of this construction Venus is at once the object of a verb in the preterite and, in pronominal form, the subject of another verb in the present tense: 'There I saw Venus, how you pray to Jupiter to protect Aeneas, since he was her son'. The sentence thus begins in the narrative mode, switches to direct address so as to bring the scene momentarily to life—it is almost as if the graven images have suddenly begun to move—and returns to narrative in the final line. In its shifts in person and tense, and its use of the concrete noun clause that prepares for them, this little scene illustrates graphic qualities of ME. syntax that it would be unfortunate to dismiss as forms of desultory expression. The impression is of a 'sensory participation in events' similar to that found by Erich Auerbach (p. 90) in the language of Gregory of Tours.

It will be for subsequent chapters to consider other ways in which Chaucer's syntax gains an effect of immediacy, and to draw attention to general features of ME. usage such as a fondness for discontinuous patterns of word-order and for negative forms of emphatic expression. My purpose here has been to suggest the kind of attention which it seems profitable to give to the syntax of medieval poetry. A possible objection to some of the comments that have been made on certain passages is that the stylistic effects claimed for them might not have been noticed by Chaucer's audience. The objection is a familiar one in the study of earlier literature, and is anticipated by Allan Rodway in a lively analysis of syntactical procedures in Augustan poetry and prose:

> But could the contemporary audience be expected to register such a variety of syntactical effects, even subconsciously? Almost certainly, yes. As a conversationalist—particularly in the Restoration period—the educated Augustan aimed at elegance and wit, and lay awake at night preparing spontaneous epigrams for the morrow. Naturally, this characteristic concern with style appeared in a higher degree in his written prose. That it should involve a play of syntax was almost inevitable. (p. 61)

We need go no further than Pandarus to find an educated courtier with as keen a sense of style in the fourteenth century, though for 'elegance and wit' read 'persuasion' and for 'epigrams' read 'platitudes'. There is, moreover, the evidence of Chaucer's poetry itself, which implies a sophisticated audience 'quick to catch the refinements of the subtlest humour and the finest irony' (Bronson, p. 53). When it is remembered that they were more used to listening than to reading, it becomes even more likely that they would have been responsive to the syntactical refinements which poetry intended for oral delivery can offer in place of metaphor and other devices of concentrated poetic expression. The anonymous fifteenth-century author of the *Book of Courtesy* was doubtless expressing a common opinion when he remarked of Chaucer that

> His language was so fayr and pertynente
> It semeth unto mannys heerynge
> Not only the worde, but verely the thynge.
> (Burrow 1969, p. 44)

The comment is as applicable to syntax as to vocabulary, and it suggests a mimetic function of language that was much appreciated by earlier readers. As Sir Francis Beaumont was to say of Chaucer later in the sixteenth century, 'one gift he hath above other authors, and that is by excellency of his descriptions to possess his readers with a more forcible imagination of seeing that (as it were) done before their eyes which they read, than any other that ever hath written in any tongue' (Burrow 1969, p. 54).

It remains to mention that the present study of Chaucer's usage attempts to avoid a narrowly descriptive approach, which isolates the language under discussion from the linguistic and literary traditions in which it was written. Reference to contemporary and earlier literature helps to reduce the risk of regarding constructions as idiosyncratic when in fact they are part of the common stock of the language, and in a more positive way it enables us to appreciate all the more those occasions on which an ordinary turn of phrase is given a special twist. In providing a measure of comparative and historical information I have made particular use, in later chapters, of F. Th. Visser's lavishly illustrated history of English syntax, which for the first time provides the student of sentences with a range of material that has long been available to the student of words. Of course, there is a limit to the amount of subsidiary matter than can reasonably be introduced into the study of a single author, and it is partly for this reason that special reference is made to the ME. rhyming romances. Little account will be taken of the possibility of foreign influence on Chaucer's syntax, which in any case can easily be over-estimated. The other reason for giving particular attention to the romances is that they are now seen to represent a native tradition of narrative poetry that exerted a measurable influence on Chaucer. They have been described as 'the source of his first poetic nourishment' (Brewer, p. 4); and it is not unreasonable to expect that he should have absorbed from them, besides such self-contained units as oaths and tags, elements of a vigorous poetic syntax that was eminently adapted to the purpose of concrete and emphatic expression.

measurable? No attempt
to measure it.

Brewer's evidence that
popular romances were
his first poetic nourishment?

9

CHAPTER II

Word-Order

Word-order makes an important contribution to style in poetry. The order of words may be emphatic, by giving prominence to a particular word or notion; it may serve a mimetic function, by tracing a sequence of events or by suggesting some other form of action; or it may simply be aesthetically pleasing for its own sake, by conveying an impression of parallelism or antithesis or by acting with the sound and rhythm of the verse to suggest a certain cadence. Many of the constructions described in the present chapter will be seen to secure effects such as these. Other constructions have been included which, though perhaps less remarkable in themselves or in their use on particular occasions, have a cumulative value in testifying to Chaucer's predilection for certain kinds of arrangement.

The description of word-order may be undertaken with reference either to grammatical units such as the parts of speech and parts of the sentence, or to recurrent patterns and processes in the ordering of words. The first method proceeds from a unit to the patterns in which it occurs; the second, which will be followed in this chapter, proceeds from a pattern to the units which it organises. My intention is to illustrate a range of constructions within such general categories as front order, broken order, cross order, and tag order, which derive in the main from Sweet's brief outline of English word-order (pp. 1–28). The advantage of this procedure, which does not pretend to offer a full scheme of analysis, is that it permits a measure of freedom in the choice and treatment of material and enables us to give particular attention to structural features that have a special relevance to the study of Chaucer's style.

Since we shall not be directly concerned with the various positions occupied by the parts of speech or with permutations of the common order subject + verb + object, it is appropriate here to mention some studies of Chaucer's word-order in which these matters are dealt with. Andrew MacLeish, for example, has undertaken 'to describe the word-order norm in the prose Subject-Verb cluster' in late fourteenth-century writings, with principal reference to Chaucer, and to compare 'the ways in which the poetic norm deviates from that of prose' (p. 11). This detailed study serves to confirm a general impression that forms of inversion and transposition are more frequent in Chaucer's poetry than in his prose; but perhaps its major contribution is to illustrate recurrent patterns of deviation from the common order and to establish the bounds within which deviations were permitted, thereby providing evidence to refute any claim that ME. writers, especially the poets, enjoyed a freedom of word-order amounting to licence. W. Weese similarly concludes that, with the exception of certain adjectival constructions and forms of transposition restricted to poetic usage, Chaucer's poetry and prose do not greatly differ in the varieties of word-order which are to be found. Having dealt with the main elements of sentence-structure, the author goes on to explore the stylistic functions of word-order in its relation to metre and rhyme; and there is a useful appendix in which attention is drawn to the essentially English character of Chaucer's phraseology, with reference to the early rhyming romances. Although this survey remains unpublished, some of the same ground is covered by Michio Masui in a comprehensive study of the relationship between word-order and rhyme in Chaucer's poetry. The use in rhyme of the parts of speech is described in detail, and some attention is given also to forms of separation and transposition.

Something of the flexibility available to Chaucer in ordering his sentences may be gauged from a well-known passage in *The Knight's Tale* that is often cited for its use of alliteration:

> In goon the speres ful sadly in arest;
> In gooth the sharpe spore into the syde.
> Ther seen men who kan juste and who kan ryde;
> Ther shyveren shaftes upon sheeldes thikke;
> He feeleth thurgh the herte-spoon the prikke.
> Up spryngen speres twenty foot on highte;
> Out goon the swerdes as the silver brighte;
> The helmes they tohewen and toshrede;
> Out brest the blood with stierne stremes rede;
> With myghty maces the bones they tobreste.
> He thurgh the thikkeste of the throng gan threste;
> Ther stomblen steedes stronge, and doun gooth al;
> He rolleth under foot as dooth a bal;
> He foyneth on his feet with his tronchoun,
> And he hym hurtleth with his hors adoun.   (*KnT* 2602–16)

A. C. Spearing remarks that in this graphic description of the tournament

the imagery is of the simplest and most conventional—the swords are as bright as silver, an unhorsed knight rolls underfoot like a ball—and there is little dislocation of natural word-order, and no muscular straining of the sense across the gap between one line and the next, such as we might expect to find in a more recent

11

poem. The genius of the passage lies in the selection of incident, the cinematic rapidity of movement between mass effects and individual sufferings (expressed grammatically in the variation between plural and singular forms), and above all in Chaucer's use of the methods of alliterative poetry. (1972, p. 19)

It is also part of Chaucer's achievement to give the impression that 'there is little dislocation of natural word-order', when in fact three-quarters of the sentences depart from the common order. Clearly, in a passage where all but one of the lines consist of a simple sentence, some structural variation is necessary so as to avoid monotony. This is duly provided by inversions, many of which, appropriately enough in a description of violent activity, draw the verb closer to the beginning of both the sentence and the line of verse. This arrangement secures variety and emphasis, and contributes to a pattern whereby in eleven of the fifteen lines, including those whose sentences are in normal order, the second place is occupied by a verb. The front-shifting of locative adverbs is the dominant type of inversion; in others the object is thrown into front position, as in 'The helmes they tohewen and toshrede', or into mid-position, as in 'And he hym hurtleth with his hors adoun', which neatly brings the combatants face to face. Yet there is no straining after novelty in these departures from the common order; variety is achieved as much by carefully interweaving the different structures and by moving prepositional phrases from one position to another through the passage (notice, for example, the suggestive chiasmus in lines 2610–11). In short, we may agree with Mr Spearing that the word-order does not call attention to itself, but it is at least as important as the alliteration in its contribution to the style of the passage. The harmonious blend of variation and repetition in the ordering of sentences contributes to an impression of violence kept firmly in check, just as each sentence marshals its forces within a single line of verse.

FRONT ORDER

In groups or sentences composed of more than two words we distinguish front-, mid-, and end-position, the last two being included under non-initial position. Thus a verb at the end of a sentence is said to have end-position: such a verb may be called an 'end-verb'. If such a verb were put at the beginning of the sentence, it would be called a 'front-shifted' verb. (Sweet, p. 1)

In this section we shall consider first some forms of front-shifting, then some negative constructions according to the element in front position, and lastly some forms of displacement. Since front position is also a feature of other types of word-order to be discussed later in this chapter, the treatment of certain constructions will be deferred until then.

The general effect of front-shifting is to give special emphasis to a word, which is usually the front-shifted item itself but can sometimes be another word in the sentence. Both of these possibilities are realised in the passage from *The Knight's Tale* that we have just been considering, where the front-shifting of locative adverbs causes an obligatory inversion that draws the verbs forward in the sentence for special effect. A word remains to be said about the front-shifted adverbs themselves. For one thing, they help to convey an impression of vigorous activity; indeed, so forceful are they that on four occasions Chaucer can afford to resort to the colourless verb *go*. Their prominence also calls attention to an impressionistic pattern of horizontal and vertical movement that is highly appropriate to the description of a *mêlée*: spurs dig *in*, spears spring *up*, blood bursts *out*, knights and their horses fall *down*. This is in keeping with the use of other syntactical features, such as the personal pronoun *he* in a demonstrative function, to suggest general rather than particular effects.

Lexical Verbs

Finite forms of lexical verbs (that is, verbs other than auxiliaries of tense or mood) are front-shifted with moderate frequency in Chaucer's poetry. The following account excludes instances of the verb *quod* 'said', whose use in this respect is stylistically unremarkable.

KnT 2743. Swelleth the brest of Arcite, and the soore / Encreesseth

KnT 2806. Dusked his eyen two, and failled breeth

KnT 2817. Shrighte Emelye, and howleth Palamon

NPT 3383. Ran Colle oure dogge, and Talbot and Gerland

The inversion in the last example is contextually appropriate, and it also serves a practical function in avoiding the top-heaviness of structure in sentences having an extended compound subject and a minimal predicate, though Chaucer normally prefers to meet this difficulty with a form of broken order. Of particular interest is the cluster of instances from the description of Arcite's death in *The Knight's Tale*, where it would appear that verbal front position has been deliberately chosen to contribute to the emotional impact of the scene. All three examples are co-ordinate constructions; in the first there is a rhetorical chiasmus which effects a striking cadence, while in the others both verbs are front-shifted for greater emphasis.

Several examples of front-shifted finite verbs are to be found in *Troilus and Criseyde*, particularly when the pace of the narrative quickens towards the end of Book II. Five stanzas in close proximity begin with this form of inversion, and a sixth with a front-shifted infinitive:

1562. Com ek Criseyde, al innocent of this

1576. Compleyned ek Eleyne of his siknesse

1590. Herde al this thyng Criseyde wel inough

1618. Answerde of this ech werse of hem than other

1625. Spak than Eleyne, and seyde

1639. To smylen of this gan tho Troilus

R. W. V. Elliott suggests that the inversion in line 1590 'is presumably simply a metrical matter, because neither *herde* nor the vague phrase "al this thyng" are sufficiently trenchant to call for emphatic positioning' (p. 70); but this is to neglect the pattern to which the line contributes. These inversions testify to a mounting sense of urgency as the plan to ensnare Criseyde takes effect in the dinner at Deiphobus' house. The movement of this section of the poem, which begins with the arrival of Criseyde ('Com ek Criseyde'), is defined by the narrator's brisk imperative: 'lat us faste go / Right to th'effect' (1565–6). Yet 'th'effect' is hidden from those taking part in the ensuing conversation—Criseyde is not alone in being 'al innocent' of what Pandarus intends—and there is thus a trace of irony in the emphasis given to the front-shifted verbs charting the flow of earnest discussion, with each of the characters eager to assert his position or record what is said.

Book II ends on a note of suspense: 'O myghty God, what shal he seye?' (1757). It is appropriate, then, that the narrative should resume in the following book with a front-shifted verb to reflect the continuity of action—or rather, since it refers to Troilus, inaction: 'Lay al this mene while Troilus' (III.50). Subsequent examples of front-shifting in the poem occur sporadically for particular local effects, and do not belong to a pattern of the kind suggested in the dinner scene:

> III.183. Fil Pandarus on knees
> IV.228. Lith Troilus, byraft of ech welfare
> IV.579. Encressen ek the causes of my care
> IV.855. Tornede hire tho Criseyde
> IV.946. Goth Pandarus, and Troilus he soughte
> IV.1085. Com Pandare in, and seyde as ye may here
> V.1646. Stood on a day in his malencolie / This Troilus

Non-finite forms of lexical verbs are also front-shifted in Chaucer's poetry. Infinitives, for example, occur in front position occasionally and with particular force:

> *Mars* 98. Fle wolde he not, ne myghte himselven hide
>
> *Tr* V.1436. Encressen gan the wo fro day to nyght / Of Troilus, for tarying of Criseyde; / And lessen gan his hope and ek his myght
>
> *Tr* V.1618. Come I wole; but yet in swich disjoynte / I stonde as now, that what yer or what day / That this shal be, that kan I naught apoynte

Criseyde's resolve in the last example illustrates emphatic usage, which on this occasion is immediately weakened by qualification. In the other examples inversion helps to point a contrast between verbs in cross order and parallel order respectively. Participles too may be front-shifted, with either verbal or adjectival force:

14

FormAge 49. Unforged was the hauberk and the plate

Tr V.1310. Acorded ben to this conclusioun, / And that anon, thise
    ilke lordes two

GenProl 89. Embrouded was he, as it were a meede   *the sequence*

GenProl 91. Syngynge he was, or floytynge, al the day   *here*

GenProl 621. Tukked he was as is a frere aboute

MillT 3263. Wynsynge she was, as is a joly colt

MLT 148. Sojourned han thise merchantz in that toun

MkT 2759. Anhanged was Cresus, the proude kyng

Scog 1. Tobroken been the statutz hye in hevene

The variation in the placing of a pronominal subject with a front-shifted
participle or adjective is governed by the principle of avoiding a heavy
stress on pronouns. Thus in the examples above we find 'Embrouded
was he', with complete inversion, beside 'Tukked he was', where a
parisyllabic participle effecting trochaic reversal draws the pronominal
subject next to it. The stylistic functions of front-shifted participles are
similar to those of predicate adjectives, to which we shall now turn. *plural*

Predicate Adjectives

The front-shifting of a predicate adjective qualifying the subject of a
sentence is a very common feature of Chaucer's descriptive verse. Here
are some representative examples from *The General Prologue*:

93. Short was his gowne, with sleves longe and wyde

99. Curteis he was, lowely, and servysable

250. Curteis he was and lowely of servyse

290. Ful thredbare was his overeste courtepy

312. Discreet he was and of greet reverence

332. Whit was his berd as is the dayesye

458. Boold was hir face, and fair, and reed of hewe

468. Gat-tothed was she, soothly for to seye

479. But riche he was of hooly thoght and werk

This word-order is sometimes found in OE. poetry (*Maldon* 111 'Biter
wæs se beaduræs') and more commonly in OFr. ('Clers fut li jurs et bels
fut li soleilz'), but it seems to have been little used in the ME. rhyming
romances and in Chaucer's own octosyllabic verse. The mildly emphatic
nature of the inversion may be judged from Chaucer's frequent use, in
his later poetry, of the adjective *greet* in front position:

Tr IV.897. 'Gret is my wo', quod she, and sighte soore

Tr V.1744. Gret was the sorwe and pleynte of Troilus

KnT 2483. Greet was the feeste in Atthenes that day

15

KnT 2989. Greet was th'effect, and heigh was his entente

MLT 393. Greet was the prees, and riche was th'array

MLT 1067. Greet was the pitee for to heere hem pleyne

WBT 1083. Greet was the wo the knyght hadde in his thoght

SqT 189. Greet was the prees that swarmeth to and fro

The sets of examples given so far illustrate the use of front-shifting to draw attention to personal features and to emphasise magnitude. Another context in which it tends to occur is in the description of lightness and darkness:

PF 263. Derk was that place, but afterward lightnesse / I saw a lyte

Mars 120. Derk was this cave, and smokyng as the helle

KnT 1062. Bright was the sonne and cleer that morwenynge

KnT 1683. Cleer was the day, as I have toold er this

MillT 3731. Derk was the nyght as pich, or as the cole

MLT 554. Bright was the sonne as in that someres day

MerchT 2219. Bright was the day, and blew the firmament

But it is difficult to generalise about such a common form of inversion, which may provide semantic emphasis or simply, since the majority of front-shifted predicate adjectives effect trochaic reversal in the first foot, a pleasing cadence. Further examples will be found below in the treatment of broken order.

Negative Constructions

It was mentioned earlier that the effect of front-shifting may be to throw the emphasis on some other word in a sentence; this is so in a variety of negative constructions where verbal inversion is used to give prominence to the negative element. Lexical verbs, for example, are occasionally front-shifted for this purpose:

Havelok 672. Eteth he neure more bred

Havelok 766. Kam he neuere hom hand-bare

Havelok 898. Sparede he neyþer tos ne heles

MkT 2011. Hadde nevere worldly man so heigh degree

More common, especially in the rhyming romances, is the front-shifting of a form of the copula *be* (usually the preterite *was* or the proclitic form *nas*):

Havelok 1638. Was neuere non so dere sold

Amis 2090. Was noman þat aboute him stode / þat durst legge on him hond

Isumbras 608. Was non so dowghty unthur schelde

PP B VIII.6. Was neuere wiȝte, as I went that me wisse couthe /
   Where this lede lenged

CA V.3820. Was non so glad of alle as sche

BD 307. Was nevere herd so swete a steven   *aux* [handwritten]

Tr I.174. Nas nevere yet seyn thyng to ben preysed derre — *aux* [handwritten]

Tr I.977. Was nevere man or womman yet bigete / That was unapt — *aux* [handwritten]
   to suffren loves hete

RvT 3957. Was noon so hardy that wente by the weye / That with
   hire dorste rage or ones pleye

MkT 2019. Was nevere swich another as was hee ·——

CYT 1342. Was nevere brid gladder agayn the day

KQuair 60. is non estate nor age / Ensured

[handwritten margin note: *No notice of exact same pattern in 2 stanzas running.*]

Front-shifted auxiliary verbs in negative sentences also occur frequently
in the romances and rather less frequently in Chaucer's poetry:

[handwritten margin note: *Beelkonde I 1582*]

Havelok 809. Shal ich neuere lengere dwelle

Amis 912. Miȝt noman morn mare

Emaré 537. Durste no mon come her hende

Tr II.754. Shal noon housbonde seyn to me 'chek mat!'

Tr IV.1200. Shal nevere lovere seyn that Troilus / Dar nat, for fere,
   with his lady dye

Here, as in the other forms of construction that have been illustrated, the
word-order is the same as that in interrogative sentences, but the presence of a negative element prevents any possibility of misunderstand-
ing. In addition, front-shifted auxiliary verbs may themselves be
preceded by the negative particle *ne*:

Havelok 1093. Ne shulde he hauen of Engellond / Onlepi forw in
   his hond

Havelok 1122. Ne shalt þou hauen non oþer king

LGW F 553. Ne shal no trewe lover come in helle

FranklT 984. Ne shall I nevere been untrewe wyf

When emphatic negative constructions such as these are considered
beside those in normal order, it will be appreciated that there was a fairly
wide scope for the expression of negation in ME. Yet so far we have seen
only one corner of the picture. The same forms of inversion also occur,
for example, with the unemphatic particle *there* to produce another set of
variations. Most of these are now obsolete, such as the use of *there* in
clauses having a lexical verb:

HF 647. And noght oonly fro fer contree / That ther no tydynge
   cometh to thee

Ven 35. Ther doth no wyght nothing so resonable

Tr IV. 1646. For in this world ther lyveth lady non, / If that ye were untrewe (as God defende!), / That so bitraised were or wo-bigon

KnT 2843. 'Right as ther dyed nevere man,' quod he, / 'That he ne lyvede in erthe in some degree, / Right so ther lyvede never man,' he seyde, / 'In al this world, that som tyme ne deyde'

SecNT 18. Of whiche ther nevere comth no good n'encrees

The last example is the clearest as a negative form of the construction with an intransitive verb that is common throughout the history of English, as in *SqT* 81 'Ther cam a knyght upon a steede of bras'. Of the others, the first is decidedly peculiar in its placing of the subject before the verb. This may represent a drastically elliptical form of 'ther (is) no tydynge (that) cometh to thee', which would make the preceding clause elliptical also: 'And (hit is) noght oonly fro fer contree'. On the other hand, the sentence may simply be anacoluthic through the insertion of *that* in line 648.

The only one of the many negative constructions under consideration to survive to the present day is that in which *there* precedes a form of the copula *be*, as in *MkT* 2072 'Ther was no boond with which men myghte him bynde'. This is much more common in Chaucer's poetry than the corresponding form without the introductory particle, as is the use of *there* in clauses having a front-shifted auxiliary verb:

Isumbras 23. There kowthe no man hit discrye

Octavian 1152. There durste noghte one habyde

PP B VI.320. there wolde none of hem chyde

Tr II.202. That, as that day, ther dorste non withstonde

Tr II.1050. Than were I ded, ther myghte it nothyng weyve

Tr IV.1197. Ther shal no deth me fro my lady twynne

Tr V.146. For trewely, ther kan no wyght yow serve

MerchT 1638. Ther may no man han parfite blisses two

SqT 141. So openly that ther shal no thyng hyde

MkT 2268. Ther myghte no thyng in hir armes stonde

CYT 1431. Ther may no man mercurie mortifie

Gent 16. But ther may no man, as men may wel see, / Bequethe his heir his vertuous noblesse

Malory 95/3. and that tyme there myght no man withstonde hym

An extra degree of emphasis is gained by restoring the subject to front position, with *there* following the auxiliary verb as a seeming redundancy:

Athelston 473. Preest schal þer non syngge

Tr III.1538. But slep ne may ther in his herte synke

18

The object of a transitive verb may also be front-shifted, with *there* coming either before or after the auxiliary:

Athelston 475. Chrystyndom schal þer non haue

CA III.235. Bot his horrible crualte / Ther mihte attempre no pite

WBT 999. A fouler wight ther may no man devyse

FranklT 1417. My body, at the leeste way, / Ther shal no wight defoulen, if I may

But this does not complete the picture of emphatic negation in sentences whose verb is typically inverted. Certain minor variations of the patterns outlined above have not been mentioned, and we have yet to consider more fully the various forms of negative existential sentences with relative clauses (Chapter 6). All such constructions make an obvious contribution to the intensive note struck in a wide range of ME. poetry, particularly in the romances.

Displacement

Before we leave the topic of front order, it will be convenient to mention some forms of displacement in subordinate and co-ordinate clauses— that is, the shifting of a word or phrase from a clause to a position immediately before the subordinating or co-ordinating conjunction. Displacement normally occurs in subordinate clauses, as in *BD* 1131 'To hire which was your firste speche', where the prepositional phrase 'to hire' precedes the relative pronoun. The construction is common in the romances and is found at least as late as Spenser: *Faerie Queene* I.x.41 'And comfort those, in point of death which lay'. The displaced element is most often a prepositional phrase:

Amis 1381. In to þe palais when þai were gon

Orfeo A 536. þurth a wildernes as y ȝede

Wynnere 101. The kyng biddith a beryn by hym þat stondeth

Emaré 5. In thy blys that we may wone

CA VIII.2224. Ferst to Nature if that I me compleigne

PF 342. The jelous swan, ayens his deth that syngeth

Tr II.485. That in this proces if ye depper go

LGW 2362. And in a cave how that she was brought

KnT 2422. The rynges on the temple dore that honge

MLT 288. I trowe at Troye, whan Pirrus brak the wal

SumT 1896. Into the temple whan they sholde gon

PrT 549. To scoleward and homward whan he wente

It will be seen from these examples that displacement occurs with most kinds of subordinate clauses. In some instances the addition of a pleonastic preposition to the end of a sentence suggests that the original force of the construction was no longer felt, perhaps as a result of over-use: *Athelston* 121 'ȝiff it be þi wille, / To chaumbyr þat þou woldest wenden tylle'. This form of pleonasm does not occur in Chaucer's poetry.

The displacement of noun phrases in the objective relation is also quite common:

> *Havelok* 856. no cold þat þu ne fonge
>
> *HarlLyr* 9.27. hire comely mouth þat mihte cusse
>
> *LybDes* C 89. þat ferst fyȝte yf Y had
>
> *Octavian* 1753. The tale whoso redyth ryght
>
> *GGK* 1647. Such chaffer and ȝe drowe
>
> *Tr* II.977. A thousand Troyes whoso that me yave
>
> *Tr* V.645. This song whan he thus songen hadde
>
> *WBT* 981. The remenant of the tale if ye wol heere
>
> *FrT* 1606. This wyde world thogh that I sholde wynne

The displacement of complements occurs rather less frequently in Chaucer's poetry:

> *Amis* 624. Mi broþer þei he were
>
> *Launfal* 279. Dame Tryamour þat hyȝte
>
> *LybDes* C 1358. Vn-crystenede þat [Y] were
>
> *Patience* 270. Relande in by a rop, a rode þat hym þoȝt
>
> *PF* 267. Hyre gilte heres with a golden thred / Ibounden were, untressed as she lay
>
> *Tr* III.170. A kynges sone although ye be, ywys
>
> *LGW* 1969. The kynges doughter, Adryane that highte

The construction is still current in concessive expressions when the complement is a predicate adjective: 'Strong as/though he is, he cannot win'. Other forms of displacement in subordinate clauses may be mentioned more briefly: for instance, of a past participle in *SqT* 335 'Enformed whan the kyng was of that knyght', and of a genitive phrase in the following examples:

> *Athelston* 574. Sere, off gylt and þay be clene
>
> *SqT* 678. Of eloquence that shal be thy peere
>
> *FranklT* 1319. But of my deeth thogh that ye have no routhe

But the displacement of an infinitive, as in *Amis* 489 'Help hir ȝif hye may' and *GGK* 1853 'þer is no haþel vnder heuen tohewe hym þat myȝt', does not seem to occur in Chaucer's poetry.

The general effect of these forms of displacement is to give the dis-placed element special emphasis. Although they are by no means limited to verse written in the high style, they may be used on such occasions for artistic effect, as in the invocation at the beginning of *Anelida and Arcite*:

> For hit ful depe is sonken in my mynde,
> With pitous hert in Englyssh to endyte
> This olde storie, *in Latyn* which I fynde.   (8–10)

> Be favorable eke, thou Polymya,
> *On Parnaso* that with thy sustres glade,
> By Elycon, not fer from Cirrea,
> Singest with vois memorial in the shade.   (15–18)

Here two prepositional phrases are displaced in relative clauses. The displacement of 'in Latyn' in line 10 neatly parallels the inversion of 'in Englyssh' in the preceding line so as to bring these complementary phrases into relief. The second example of displacement is perhaps more forceful in belonging to a sentence whose verb is delayed until a line which C. S. Lewis felt 'to contain within itself the germ of the whole central tradition of high poetical language in England' (p. 201).

One form of displacement remains to be considered, in co-ordinate clauses introduced by *and*. In *Alisaunder* B 7530 'Ygreiþed ben þis foure þousynde / Quyklick and on hors wende', for example, the adverb *quyklich* belongs with the following verb ('and rode off quickly on horseback'). This romance provides the earliest recorded instances of the 'inverted *and*' construction (see Bennett and Smithers, p. 278), but there are several examples later in Gower's poetry:

CA III.222. And sche began merci to crie, / Upon hire bare knes and preide

CA VIII.2460. Min yhe and as I caste aboutes

Macaulay (vol. 1, p. 460) in his note on the first of these examples gives other instances and refers to a similar form of displacement before *et* in Gower's French verse. Compare the following sentences from Chaucer's octosyllabic verse, in which an adjunct coming between two verbs may be taken with either verb:

BD 769. Al this I putte in his servage, / As to my lord and dide homage

HF 1663. hit mote be knowe, / Ryght as hit is and forth yblowe

I have altered the editorial punctuation of these lines to suggest a possible interpretation. In the first example especially it makes better sense to construe the phrase 'as to my lord' with 'dide homage' than with 'putte in his servage', though the resemblance to the 'inverted *and*' construction may be coincidental. The origin of this curious form of expression remains a mystery.

21

But broken order is often suspension; see bot 23 etc.

ⅠⅠ   BROKEN ORDER

Broken order is very frequent in Old-English. When two or more co-ordinate words ought to precede a word which they jointly modify or are modified by, there is a tendency to avoid suspensiveness by putting only one of them before this word, and letting the others follow in tag-order: *swiþe micle meras fersce* 'very large fresh-water lakes' | *Cynewulf benam Sigebryht his rices and Westseaxna witan* 'Cynewulf and the West-Saxon senators deprived Sigebryht of his kingdom' | *gesæt þæt land and gedælde* 'occupied the country and divided it' . . . Modern English is much more tolerant of suspensiveness, and the logical spirit of the language makes it averse to broken order. The Old-English order adjective + noun + adjective survives only in such isolated phrases as *good men and true.*   (Sweet, pp. 24–5)

Broken order is a special form of discontinuity in which the separated elements are co-ordinate; other forms of discontinuity will be considered in a later section. Sweet's examples from OE. prose illustrate the broken order of attributive adjectives, subjects, and verbs respectively. These and other kinds of broken order are found in ME. poetry, some of them with considerable frequency. Behind them may lie a general desire to avoid suspensiveness, but we shall also have to consider their use in securing emphasis and other special effects, their practical convenience, and their relation to metre and rhyme.

Subjects and Objects

The fondness of ME. writers for broken order is perhaps nowhere more evident than in the placing of two co-ordinate noun phrases in the subjective relation, one before and one after the predicate, so as to yield sentences like 'The man came and his son'. It is sometimes suggested that such sentences illustrate a stage in the history of English between primitive repetition ('The man came and his son came') and modern contraction ('The man and his son came'), but this explanation is doubly misleading. First, although the broken order of subjects becomes less common in MnE., in no sense does it belong to a stage of linguistic history, for the contracted form is found beside it in all periods of the language. It belongs instead to a stage in the history of style, as do the other forms of broken order. Secondly, it would be wrong to infer that the 'intermediate' form was effected by ellipsis of the second verb; this form is simply a rearrangement of the same elements found in a sentence having a compound subject in normal order.

   The broken order of subjects may be used to satisfy metrical requirements and generally to secure balance and emphasis. Consideration must also be given to what Quirk and Greenbaum call 'the principle of end-weight', which is the tendency in English 'to reserve the final position for the more complex parts of a clause or sentence' (p. 410). The top-heavy structure of a sentence like 'The man and his son, who was twelve years of age, came', for example, might be reformed in ME. usage by placing the verb immediately after the first noun.

22

Co-ordinate noun phrases and pronouns in the subjective relation are most often separated by a verb phrase, which may take some form of adjunct:

Havelok 2976. hwar-of no lathe / Mihte rise, ne no wrathe

Amis 520. Hir moder com wiþ diolful chere / & al þe leuedis þat þer were

Orfeo A 89. Kniʒtes vrn & leuedis also

PP B VIII.88. That the erl Auarous helde, and his heires

HF 159. and kyng Pryam yslayn / And Polytes, his sone, certayn

HF 454. And alle the batayles that hee / Was at hymself, and eke hys knyghtis

Tr I.804. Thus wol she sayn, and al the town attones

Tr III.1710. And whan hire speche don was and hire cheere

Tr IV.1560. If this were wist, my lif lay in balaunce, / And youre honour

LGW 2610. The torches brennen, and the laumpes bryghte

SumT 1863. And up I roos, and al oure covent eke

MerchT 1617. Placebo cam, and eek his freendes soone

MerchT 1914. I wol myself visite hym, and eek May

The practical advantage of the construction in avoiding problems of agreement is to be seen in *HF* 454–5. This word-order may be used to emphasise the second subject or, conversely, to suggest that it is an afterthought. In saying to Troilus 'my lif lay in balaunce, / And youre honour', which of the two considerations has Criseyde uppermost in her thoughts?

Most of the examples above illustrate a fairly simple form of broken order in single lines of verse, but more complex patterns also occur in Chaucer's poetry:

BD 53. That clerkes had in olde tyme, / And other poets, put in rime

NPT 3219. Into the yerd ther Chauntecleer the faire / Was wont, and eek his wyves, to repaire

In these examples the predicate itself is split in two by the insertion of the second subject. This is a more forceful kind of discontinuity, which seems to relegate the second subject to an inferior, parenthetical position. The double discontinuity in *BD* 53–4 suggests something of the narrator's casual response to a book which he takes up only to 'drive the night away' (49). The construction in the second example is also suggestive. In this brief description of the farmyard the word-order mimes the progress of the vain Chauntecleer with his nameless wives trailing behind. These hens have already been accorded inferior status by means of broken order in an earlier passage: 'And with that word he fley

23

doun fro the beem, / For it was day, and eke his hennes alle' (*NPT* 3172–3). Here too the syntax traces the order of events, and the separation of the second subject effectively establishes the hens as mere followers.

Other forms of the broken order of subjects may be noted more briefly. Discontinuity is occasionally caused by an intervening adjunct, as in *KnT* 2600 'Now ryngen trompes loude and clarioun' (though if *loude* was intended as an adjective there is no discontinuity). An asyndetic relative clause is sometimes responsible for broken order in exclamations:

> *BD* 1244. Allas! that day / The sorowe I suffred, and the woo
>
> *WBProl* 384. O Lord! the peyne I dide hem and the wo

There is one form of broken order which in certain contexts might mislead a modern reader. ME. poets frequently split a compound subject even when the verb takes an object, with the result that the end-shifted subject might itself be taken for an object:

> *Amis* 2303. God graunt me þer-to wel to spede, / & Mari, þat best may
>
> *MLT* 998. For which the senatour, as was usage, / Rood hym agayns, and many of his lynage
>
> *MLT* 1100. The morwe cam, and Alla gan hym dresse, / And eek his wyf, this Emperour to meete
>
> *MerchT* 2418. God blesse us, and his mooder Seinte Marie
>
> *PardProl* 308. God blesse hem, and oure lady Seinte Marie

In the examples of optative clauses, where broken order is often found, God is not being asked to bless Mary, just as in *MLT* 1100–1 it is not being suggested that Alla's preparations included dressing his wife.

The broken order of objects occurs in verse and prose from OE. onwards, and its effects are generally similar to those achieved by the broken order of subjects. When a verb with or without its subject is responsible for the discontinuity, the first object comes before the verb:

> *Havelok* 757. Keling he tok, and tumberel
>
> *Havelok* 1269. It bekenneth more þat he shal / Denemark hauen, and Englond al
>
> *PF* 591. Who can a resoun fynde or wit in that?
>
> *Tr* I.982. Hire beaute to bithynken and hire youthe
>
> *Tr* II.468. I shal so doon, myn honour shal I kepe, / And ek his lyf
>
> *Tr* IV.232. and every dore he shette / And wyndow ek
>
> *LGW* F 138. The foweler we deffye, / And al his craft
>
> *MkT* 2055. This Sampsoun nevere ciser drank ne wyn
>
> *CYProl* 709. Er that he dye, sorwe have he and shame

Once again Criseyde puts her own well-being before that of Troilus, using the same pair of terms that we have seen in *Tr* IV.1560–1. On this occasion, however, it is her honour that comes first and his life second. *that his life comes at all in this context is remarkable.*

Sometimes an adjunct intervenes between the two objects:

> *BD* 1195. Nature / Ne formed never in creature / So muche beaute, trewely, / And bounte
>
> *HF* 703. Though that Fame had alle the pies / In al a realme, and alle the spies
>
> *Tr* I.1064. And fynde a tyme therto, and a place

and sometimes a relative clause:

> *LGW* 1248. Swich sorwe as he hath maked, and swich cheere, / It is a routhe and pite for to here
>
> *WBProl* 786. Who wolde wene, or who wolde suppose, / The wo that in myn herte was, and pyne?

In this last example the Wife of Bath achieves a particular emphasis by using synonymous objects in broken order as part of a rhetorical question introduced twice in similar terms. The sentence is balanced and forceful, and conveys a measure of urgency.

Verbs and Adjuncts

The broken order of verbs occurs quite frequently in Chaucer's poetry. The separation is most often caused by an object, adjunct, auxiliary verb, or inverted subject, examples of which are found throughout Early English literature. Some grammarians tend to find ellipsis when examining this form of broken order. Ohlander (1943, p. 116), for instance, points to the ellipsis of an object-pronoun after the second of two co-ordinate verbs in broken order, giving as an example *Havelok* 420 'He hem [ne] cloþede riht, ne fedde'. But sentences of this kind are no more elliptical than those in which the same elements are in normal order, as in *Havelok* 2907 'þou feddes and claddes me ful wel'. Similarly, constructions of the type 'I must go and will', where the main verb comes between its auxiliaries, are simply alternative arrangements of the order 'I must and will go':

> *Tr* III.376. if I late or yerne / Wolde it bewreye, or dorst, or sholde konne
>
> *Tr* IV.216. It was for nought; it moste ben and sholde

The broken order of auxiliary verbs in these examples is an emphatic usage that occurs only rarely in Chaucer's poetry. Similar constructions in which ellipsis does occur will be considered in Chapter 5.

The order of co-ordinate lexical verbs may be broken by their common object:

Guy I A 2765. He loued hir, & worþ-schiped swiþe

Gowther 248. That he mey schryfte me and asoyll

HF 941. Whan the sonnes sone, the rede, / That highte Pheton, wolde lede / Algate hys fader carte, and gye

Tr III.1767. To cerclen hertes alle, and faste bynde

LGW F 392. For whan a flye offendeth him or biteth

FranklT 1486. That folk of yow may demen harm or gesse

More commonly, some form of adjunct intervenes:

Havelok 420. He hem [ne] cloþede riht, ne fedde

BD 872. Had made hem opene by mesure, / And close

HF 775. The air ys twyst with violence / And rent

Anel 340. But me to rede out of this drede, or guye

Tr I.984. though that hire liste bothe and kowthe

KnT 2202. Or which of hem kan dauncen best and synge

MLT 345. To lyve with hire and dye, and by hire stonde

WBProl 443. What eyleth yow to grucche thus and grone?

MerchT 1781. But there I lete hym wepe ynogh and pleyne

SqT 126. Though that ye slepen on his bak or reste

FranklT 783. Causeth ful ofte to doon amys or speken

Although Chaucer doubtless availed himself of broken order on occasion to satisfy the requirements of metre and rhyme, the evidence of such examples testifies to a partiality for this pattern of words even when other arrangements were possible. The first phrase in *MLT* 345 might easily be put in normal order (and so it is in a few manuscripts), but the resulting chiasmus of 'To lyve and dye with hire, and by hire stonde' deflects the emphasis from the verbs to the prepositional phrases and is rather less forceful.

In the forms of broken order that have so far been considered, the element responsible for discontinuity has been in normal order with the first verb (verb + object, verb + adjunct). Other forms are due to inversion, as of subject and verb:

Amis 2305. No lenger stint he no stode

KnT 2486. That al that Monday justen they and daunce

FranklT 817. For his absence wepeth she and siketh

Co-ordinate infinitives or past participles may be separated by an inverted auxiliary verb:

PF 516. Of which he neyther rede can ne synge

Tr I.838. Ne al the men that riden konne or go

Tr IV.799. How myghte it evere yred ben or ysonge?

Other elements will be found to intervene between co-ordinate verbs—a relative clause, for example, in *Lady* 60 'What have I doon that greveth yow, or sayd?'—but the varieties that have been described are the most common in Chaucer's usage.

Adjuncts less often occur in broken order. These may take the form of adverbs or prepositional phrases in which the preposition, if common to both phrases, is sometimes repeated and sometimes not. I include instances where an adverb is in broken order with a prepositional phrase:

HSynne 9117. Fellyche thou cursedest, and ouer sone

BD 852. So goodly speke and so frendly

BD 1041. And I hooly hires and everydel

Anel 275. And putte yow in sclaunder now and blame

PF 21. The longe day ful faste I redde and yerne

Tr III.1796. so wel he koude devyse / Of sentement, and in so unkouth wise

GenProl 58. At Lyeys was he and at Satalye

In the case of constructions like that in *Anel* 275 it is perhaps more accurate to say that the headwords in a compound prepositional phrase are discontinuous. The preposition is also expressed only once in *BD* 411 'That wynter, thorgh hys colde morwes, / Had mad hyt suffre, and his sorwes', which has an effect of double discontinuity. This construction may be compared with the broken order of subjects and predicative discontinuity in *BD* 53–4 mentioned above.

Complements

Co-ordinate predicate nouns and adjectives are often separated by a form of the verb *be* in ME. poetry.

Havelok 217. þat tendre was, and swiþe neysh

HarlLyr 7.31. hire lockes lefly aren ant longe

Octavian 1472. Wyth men that crafty were and gode

GGK 2047. Thenne watz Gryngolet grayþe, þat grete watz and huge

CA I.1472. This knyht, which worthi was and wys

HF 1386. Hir heer, that oundy was and crips

Tr III.408. That this servise a shame be or jape

LGW 993. Of which that Dido lady is and queen

KnT 3004. That thilke Moevere stable is and eterne

MillT 3671. This Absolon ful joly was and light

SumT 1936. But we that humble been, and chaast, and poore

SqT 48. Phebus the sonne ful joly was and cleer

Complements in broken order normally refer to the subject and only occasionally to the object, as in *LGW* F 126 'Of wynter, that hym naked

27

made and mat'. When more than one predicate noun or adjective is in end position, they may be co-ordinated, as in *SumT* 1936 above, or the first of them may directly follow the verb, as in *Tr* IV.784 'Shal sorwe ben, compleynt, and abstinence'.

The front-shifting of predicate adjectives has previously been described. Here are some examples of complements in broken order where the first is in front position before the verb and its subject:

> *GenProl* 458. Boold was hir face, and fair, and reed of hewe
> *GenProl* 591. Ful longe were his legges and ful lene
> *KnT* 1187. Greet was the strif and long bitwix hem tweye
> *KnT* 1369. So feble eek were his spiritz, and so lowe
> *SqT* 52. Ful lusty was the weder and benigne

The subject in these examples is a noun phrase, and there is inversion of subject and verb for metrical reasons. When the subject is a personal pronoun, the verb follows it in normal order:

> *Arthour* A 81. Strong he was and wiȝt ywis
> *Amis* 1395. Glad he was & fain
> *Amis* 2187. Ful trewe þai ware & kinde
> *GenProl* 626. As hoot he was and licherous as a sparwe
> *KnT* 1362. That lene he wex and drye as is a shaft
> *CYT* 746. For unto shrewes joye it is and ese

That these forms of broken order are not merely metrical expedients may be seen by comparing alternative arrangements that preserve both sense and metre. *GenProl* 626, for example, easily converts to normal order ('He was as hoot and licherous as a sparwe'), but it sacrifices something of the rhythm and emphasis of the original line.

Genitive Phrases

Certain forms of broken order involve the use of genitive phrases formed with *of*, which may either be discontinuous themselves or be responsible for discontinuity. Here first are some examples of a genitive phrase separating the two nouns which it qualifies:

> *CA* V.4035. Unto Echates the goddesse / Of art magique and the maistresse
> *BD* 911. And chef ensample of al hir werk, / And moustre
> *SqT* 309. the kyng axeth this knyght / The vertu of this courser and the myght

Chaucer sometimes uses an elliptical construction that resembles this form of broken order:

KnT 1763. He hath considered shortly, in a clause, / The trespas of
 hem bothe, and eek the cause

SumT 2196. Ye been the salt of the erthe and the savour

Although these sentences are comparable in their rhythm and structure
to instances of true broken order, a moment's reflection reveals that the
first is actually a contracted form of 'the trespas of hem bothe, and eek
the cause (of the trespas)', and the second a contracted form of 'Ye been
the salt of the erthe and the savour (of the salt)' (after Matt. v.13).

Co-ordinate nouns or adjectives having a genitive phrase in common
may be further separated by a form of the verb *be*:

PF 199. That God, that makere is of al and lord

LGW 914. That warm was of hire loves blod, and hot

KQuair 134. In ver that full of vertu is and gude

Compare the following construction in which a verb still comes between
the co-ordinate nouns but does not separate the first of them from the
genitive phrase: *SumT* 2274 'the soun of it wol wende, / And eke the
stynk'. Two genitive phrases qualifying a single noun or adjective may
themselves be separated, usually by a form of *be*:

PF 77. That ful of blysse is and of soules cleere

Tr I.608. it were a gretter joie / To me than kyng of Grece ben and
 Troye

Tr III.1037. And som so ful of furie is and despit

The preposition is normally not repeated, and in such instances it is
once again perhaps more accurate to refer to the broken order of co-
ordinate headwords in the phrase.

Attributive Adjectives

The two main forms of adjectival broken order are represented by the
colligation premodifier + noun + postmodifier, the difference between
these forms being whether or not *and* is expressed before the postmodifier. The asyndetic variety occurs sporadically in OE., as in 'swiþe
micle meras fersce' quoted by Sweet at the beginning of this section.
There are few examples in the ME. rhyming romances, and in those few
the postmodifier is usually a numeral; the widespread use of the construction in later courtly poetry is no doubt due in part to the influence
of postmodification in the Romance languages. The following list of
representative examples takes account of attributive adjectives and
numerals only:

Isumbras 279. And ryche robes sevenne

Gowther 435. Tho dompe meydon schene

BD 108. A! mercy! swete lady dere

HF 36. Or that the cruel lyf unsofte

Anel 38. With Emelye, her yonge suster shene

PF 352. That clepeth forth the grene leves newe

Tr I.470. The sharpe shoures felle of armes preve

Tr II.821. And shadewed wel with blosmy bowes grene

Tr IV.1209. And thow, Criseyde, o swete herte deere

KnT 976. So shyneth in his white baner large

KnT 2598. Do now youre devoir, yonge knyghtes proude

MLT 447. O Emperoures yonge doghter deere

MerchT 1638. Ther may no man han parfite blisses two

MerchT 2367. O stronge lady stoore, what dostow?

PardT 871. And borwed of hym large botelles thre

MkT 2100. He Arpies slow, the crueel bryddes felle

SecNT 201. An oold man, clad in white clothes cleere

Scog 3. Syth that I see the bryghte goddis sevene

This pattern of words, frequently but not invariably a feature of the high style, is very common in Chaucer's descriptive verse and was taken up by later poets like Lydgate. It is normally found at the end of a line.

The order of adjectival premodifiers is determined by a complex of structural and semantic considerations. We say, for example, 'an old yellow book' but 'a little old lady', the position of *old* depending on its relation to both the noun and the other adjective. A chart of premodification sequence such as that given by Quirk and Greenbaum (p. 404) specifies that adjectives of size precede those of age, which precede those of colour, and so on. As this sequence appears not to have changed fundamentally since the ME. period, it can be used to distinguish three basic patterns of asyndetic broken order in Chaucer's poetry:

A   white baner large   (a + x) + b

B   blosmy bowes grene   a + (x + b)

C   crueel bryddes felle   a + x + b

This analysis accords with Chaucer's usage in the placing of two adjectives before a noun. Type A is possibly the most common, and represents the postmodification of a noun phrase in normal order. Type B, the premodification of a noun phrase in inverted order, occurs somewhat less frequently, as does type C, in which there is no clear order of semantic precedence and the adjectives are thus interchangeable: in *Tr* IV.1209 Troilus addresses Criseyde as 'swete herte deere' and she replies in line 1274 with 'deere herte sweete'. Because in this last type the two adjectives are near synonyms, the construction tends to be strong and generalised in its effect. It is a common feature of the speech of lovers and is also found in the description of unpleasant objects and experiences, though this interesting duality of usage is possibly fortuitous.

Asyndetic broken order may be compared with co-ordinate postmodification in sentences like *GenProl* 93 'Short was his gowne, with sleves longe and wyde', where it is a simple matter to put the noun phrase into broken order without disrupting the metre: 'with longe sleves wyde'. By the same token, the broken order of *Tr* I.470 'The sharpe shoures felle of armes preve' is easily reformed to give co-ordinate postmodification: 'The shoures sharpe and felle of armes preve'. The interchangeability of these two constructions is conditional on the first adjective being disyllabic and ending in final-*e* before a noun beginning with a consonant. *KnT* 1302 'the asshen dede and colde', for example, cannot be put into broken order, because 'dede asshen' is metrically unacceptable.

There are several varieties of the basic asyndetic pattern premodifier + noun + postmodifier. There may be co-ordinate postmodification:

> *GenProl* 90. Al ful of fresshe floures, whyte and reede
>
> *KnT* 1755. And saugh hir blody woundes wyde and soore

or premodification by means of two or more adjectives in asyndetic co-ordination:

> *CA* V.3652. Mi worthi lusti lady dere
>
> *KnT* 1977. With knotty, knarry, bareyne trees olde
>
> *KnT* 2386. Of faire, yonge, fresshe Venus free
>
> *FranklT* 868. But, Lord, thise grisly feendly rokkes blake
>
> *SecNT* 293. Seyde this blisful faire mayde deere

These examples once again suggest meliorative/pejorative usage, with the same pattern of words being employed to describe both beautiful women and unpleasant objects. The piling up of words in asyndetic co-ordination for emphasis and emotive effect seems to be a fairly earnest widespread linguistic phenomenon (see also p. 129 below), and is used here to convey something of the speaker's attitude in awarding praise or blame. The effects achieved by this encrustation of adjectives on a noun are supported in some instances by appropriate patterns of sounds, as in the harsh consonant clusters of *KnT* 1977 and the smoothly flowing fricatives of *KnT* 2386.

The definite article is used in certain forms of asyndetic broken order when the headword is a proper noun. In the following examples the article precedes the postmodifier:

> *Tr* V.655. For which, O brighte Latona the clere
>
> *KnT* 1747. Ye shal be deed, by myghty Mars the rede
>
> *SecNT* 115. Right so was faire Cecilie the white
>
> *Ven* 43. For subtil Jelosie, the deceyvable

The function of the article is often to draw attention to a distinctive attribute by partially converting the adjective into a noun in apposition; it is a form of labelling. There is also a prosodic consideration, in that a proper noun taking or ending in a heavy stress must generally be followed by a light stress in an iambic line of verse. The use of the definite article satisfies this requirement. The opposite arrangement, with the premodifier taking the article, is also found, as in *KnT* 2215 'Unto the blisful Citherea benigne', and sometimes both adjectives take the article:

> *KnT* 2443. Til that the pale Saturnus the colde
>
> *SecNT* 177. To shewen you the goode Urban the olde

The other main type of adjectival broken order in Chaucer's poetry, represented by 'good men and true', has a long history in the language (see Kellner, pp. 300–1). It is found in OE. and throughout the ME. period in both verse and prose, usually as a feature of ordinary rather than elevated narrative:

> *Havelok* 1071. Hu he was strong man and hey
>
> *Patience* 481. With hatel anger and hot heterly he calleʒ
>
> *MandTravels* 8/32. that bare gode fruyt and blessed
>
> *Tr* I.892. Of noble corage and wel ordayné
>
> *Tr* III.1247. Hire armes smale, hire streghte bak and softe
>
> *SecNT* 351. and with glad herte and light / He cristned hym

What proportions?

In this form, however, the constuction is infrequent in Chaucer's poetry. It is more usual to find both adjectives taking the indefinite article:

> *Athelston* 60. A good kyng and a ryche
>
> *Wynnere* 74. A lighte lebarde and a longe
>
> *MandTravels* 67/28. a fair castelle and a strong
>
> *Emaré* 74. Was a curteys lorde and a gode
>
> *GenProl* 531. A trewe swynkere and a good was he
>
> *GenProl* 647. He was a gentil harlot and a kynde
>
> *MerchT* 1271. Thanne sholde he take a yong wyf and a feir
>
> *FranklT* 871. Of swich a parfit wys God and a stable
>
> *PardT* 713. An oold man and a povre with hem mette
>
> *ShipT* 25. Ther was a monk, a fair man and a boold

The use of the indefinite article with the postmodifier gives the construction an appearance of symmetry, and in verse it is necessary in order to preserve the metre. When the premodifier is a monosyllabic adjective ending in a consonant, it has the strong form without inflexion after the indefinite article in ME. Careful writers like Chaucer avoid such constructions as 'an oolde man and povre', which is metrical but ungrammatical, and 'an oold man and povre', which is grammatically correct but metrically inferior. The construction may be compared with appositive postmodification in such lines as *GenProl* 208 'A Frere ther was, a wantowne and a merye', which will be considered later in the section on tag order.

III DISCONTINUITY

Discontinuity refers to the separation of closely related words and phrases in a clause or sentence. As we have seen, broken order is a special kind of discontinuity in which the separated elements are co-ordinate. Although warnings against such misplacements as 'Wanted: armchair for old gentleman with sliding back and oak legs' and arguments about the split infinitive are familiar enough, grammarians have only recently begun to describe other forms of separation in contemporary usage, and there has been no general historical treatment. Only Masui (pp. 145–50) devotes more than passing attention to this aspect of Chaucer's syntax. Separations are more liable to occur in verse than in prose, especially in verse written according to a theory of style which promotes them as devices conducing to elevated expression. As the twelfth-century rhetorician Geoffrey of Vinsauf puts it in his *Poetria Nova*, 'Juxtaposition of related words conveys the sense more readily, but their moderate separation sounds better to the ear and has greater elegance' (p. 54). Some of the most familiar separations are forms of discontinuous modification. Discontinuous noun phrases are very common in ME. when the postponed element is a relative clause, and these will be discussed in Chapter 6. For the moment we shall be concerned with other forms of discontinuous modification: first the separation of genitive phrases from nouns and adjectives, and then the varieties of the split genitive.

α *Separated Genitive Phrases*

The separation of a genitive phrase from the noun it qualifies is a common form of discontinuity in ME. poetry. Elements of different lengths and grammatical functions may be responsible for the separation, one of the most frequent being a form of the verb *be*:

Havelok 2534. þat Hauelok king was of Denemark

Wynnere 473. þer moste waste es of wele

HF 81. And he that mover ys of al

PF 62. That welle is of musik and melodye

Tr II.443. By Neptunus, that god is of the see

Tr IV.879. That cause is of this sorwe and this unreste

LGW F 113. That in the brest was of the beste

MillT 3249. And softer than the wolle is of a wether

MLT 604. And eek Alla, that kyng was of that lond

33

MkT 2412. The eldest scarsly fyf yeer was of age

SecNT 3. That porter of the gate is of delices

KQuair 908. That corner-stone and ground is of the wall

The construction is often comparable in its rhythm to the broken order of complements. It occurs several times in *The House of Fame* (see also lines 391, 1447, 1486–7, 1512) and in *Troilus and Criseyde* when, as in the example from Book II quoted above, the genitive phrase qualifies the noun *god* (see also II.630, IV.1545, V.892).

Discontinuity is also often caused by other verbal forms, which may be accompanied by an adverbial adjunct:

HF 1113. I wol yow al the shap devyse / Of hous and site

PF 449. Another tersel egle spak anon, / Of lower kynde

Tr II.1321. But ofte gan the herte glade and quake / Of Troilus

Tr IV.1391. to don the wrathe pace / Of Priamus

GenProl 134. That in hir coppe ther was no ferthyng sene / Of grece

KnT 2261. Whan the orison was doon of Palamon

MLT 260. The day is comen of hir departynge

WBProl 115. to what conclusion / Were membres maad of generacion?

MerchT 1578. Fro day to day gan in the soule impresse / Of Januarie

SqT 466. If that I verraily the cause knewe / Of youre disese

NPT 2977. That al the revers seyn of this sentence

KQuair 900. And so the end sall turne of thy folye

Once again, separations are frequent in parts of *The House of Fame* (see also lines 951–2, 1337–8, 1507–8, 1759–60), usually in run-on lines of verse, which Masui (p. 214) mentions as a characteristic feature of the construction. It may be noted that in certain of the examples above (*Tr* II.1321, *WBProl* 116, *MerchT* 1578) an intervening infinitive or past participle is itself separated from a preceding auxiliary verb so as to give a form of double discontinuity.

More extensive forms of separation may be caused by the interposition of the major elements of sentence-structure. When both the subject and verb of a sentence intervene, the noun qualified by a genitive phrase is often a front-shifted object or complement. I include some examples of existential sentences constructed with the formal subject *there*:

Isumbras 343. Sayles they drewen up of good hewe

CA V.4016. And ek a part sche tok of leves

HF 1151. For on that other syde I say / Of this hil

Tr V.805. And heir he was of Calydoigne and Arge

LGW 768. The colde wal they wolden kysse of ston

34

GenProl 56. In Gernade at the seege eek hadde he be / Of Algezir

GenProl 285. A Clerk ther was of Oxenford also

GenProl 343. Withoute bake mete was nevere his hous / Of fissh and flessh

GenProl 477. A good man was ther of religioun

KnT 1753. For gentil men they were of greet estaat

FranklT 1124. At Orliens in studie a book he say / Of magyk natureel

ShipT 3. A wyf he hadde of excellent beautee

A verb taking an object or complement may come between the genitive phrase and its noun:

HF 524. And in the tresorye hyt shette / Of my brayn

Tr I.891. For certaynly, the firste poynt is this / Of noble courage and wel ordayné

Tr II.3. For in this see the boot hath swych travaylle, / Of my connyng, that unneth I it steere

Mars 212. The poynt is this of my distruccioun

KnT 1118. The fresshe beautee sleeth me sodeynly / Of hire that rometh in the yonder place

PrT 555. The swetnesse hath in his herte perced so / Of Cristes mooder

CYT 1315. And in the panne putte it at the laste / Of water

Chaucer appears to use this construction on some occasions to create an impression of difficulty. J. A. Burrow comments as follows on the proem to Book II of *The House of Fame*, which includes the discontinuity in lines 524–5 quoted above:

> In the address to the Muses, rhetorical periphrasis combines with abnormal word-order (inversion of verb and object, separation of pronoun from relative clause) to produce a 'difficult' effect reminiscent of Dante and Latin poetry. But the difficulty is not marked, for the diction remains simple (except in the phrase 'tresorye . . . of my brayn'); and the whole passage produces an effect more homogeneous than analysis of its parts might suggest. (1971, p. 22)

P. F. Baum is less appreciative of the discontinuity in *Tr* II.3–4, which he describes as 'awkward' and takes to indicate 'Chaucer's light-hearted view of the matter' (pp. 86–7). But the tone of the proem seems serious enough; and the function of the discontinuity, as of the emphatic placing of the adverb *unneth* 'with difficulty', is surely to reflect the narrator's professed difficulty with his 'tempestuous matere'.

Other elements responsible for discontinuity include an adverb in *BD*

35

663 'Than Athalus, that made the game / First of the ches', a direct object in *KnT* 942 'To do the dede bodyes vileynye / Of alle oure lordes', and a prepositional phrase in the following examples:

> *Tr* V.1436. Encressen gan the wo fro day to nyght / Of Troilus
>
> *KnT* 2907. With vessels in hir hand of gold ful fyn
>
> *NPT* 2874. That trewely she hath the herte in hoold / Of Chauntecleer

Relative clauses sometimes intervene:

> *BD* 1326. And the book that I hadde red, / Of Alcione and Seys the kyng
>
> *Tr* V.311. In a vessell that men clepeth an urne, / Of gold

These and other more extensive forms of separation are fairly common in Chaucer's poetry but not, so far as I have noticed, in the romances.

In accounting for the effect of discontinuity in the constructions that have so far been described, consideration must be given to such factors as the position of the genitive phrase in the line of verse, the length of the separation, and the syntactical function of the phrase. The last of these is perhaps the most important in deciding whether we are given an impression of disjunction, which tends to be conveyed more forcibly by a possessive genitive than by a descriptive genitive. Compare the following sentences:

> *GenProl* 343. Withoute bake mete was nevere his hous / Of fissh and flessh
>
> *PrT* 555. The swetnesse hath in his herte percede so / Of Cristes mooder

The length of separation is about the same in both sentences, and in both there is the characteristic enjambment; yet the second seems more disjunctive. This is possibly because a descriptive genitive, as in the first example, may have the force of an appositive construction and therefore seem less radically separated from its antecedent than does the possessive genitive in the second.

Various forms of separation also occur when the genitive phrase and its noun are transposed. Here are some representative examples:

> *Havelok* 1264. Of an angel she herde a uoyz
>
> *Octavian* 387. Of alle kyngys thou art flowre
>
> *Emaré* 209. That of golde wered the crowne
>
> *CA* I.256. Bot next above alle othre schewe / Of love I wol the propretes
>
> *BD* 250. Of down of pure dowves white / I wil yive hym a fether-bed
>
> *HF* 130. Hyt was of Venus redely / The temple

Tr V.1752. Of Troilus, this ilke noble knyght, / As men may in
thise olde bokes rede, / Was seen his knyghthod and his grete
myght

LGW 2244. Of Trace was he lord, and kyn to Marte

GenProl 75. Of fustian he wered a gypon

KnT 1440. That of his chambre he made hym a squier

WBProl 107. But Crist, that of perfeccion is welle

MkT 2497. For of moralitee he was the flour

In general, discontinuous constructions seem less forcibly disjunctive
when the genitive phrase is transposed, because the inversion creates an
expectation that is not fulfilled until the noun to which the phrase refers
is reached. When the separated elements are in normal order, the syntactical suspense is considerably reduced; and, if these elements are some
distance apart, the genitive phrase may come as a surprise. On the reinforcement of the construction by means of a possessive adjective in
Tr V.1752–4 see p. 77 below.

Chaucer's frequent use of discontinuous modification in *The House of
Fame* has already been mentioned. Certain forms of discontinuity tend
to be concentrated in particular sections of the poem, especially in the
description of the 'folk of digne reverence' who stand on pillars in the
palace of Fame. Separated genitive phrases are used three times in
succession to describe the pillars occupied by Ovid, Lucan, and
Claudian:

> And next hym on a piler was,
> Of coper, Venus clerk, Ovide. (1486–7)

> Thoo saugh I on a piler by,
> Of yren wroght ful sternely,
> The grete poete, daun Lucan. (1497–9)

> And next him on a piler stood
> Of soulfre, lyk as he were wood,
> Daun Claudian, the sothe to telle. (1507–9)

Shortly before this the achievements of Joseph, Statius, and Virgil have
been described in sentences employing a discontinous phrasal verb:

> And he *bar* on hys shuldres hye
> The fame *up* of the Jewerye. (1435–6)

> The Tholosan that highte Stace,
> That *bar* of Thebes *up* the fame
> Upon his shuldres, and the name
> Also of cruel Achilles. (1460–3)

37

> The Latyn poete, Virgile,
> That *bore* hath *up* a longe while
> The fame of Pius Eneas. (1483–5)

For the normal order compare *HF* 1439 'To helpen him bere up the charge' and lines 1490, 1500–2, 1510. In fact there is double discontinuity in all three examples above, since the elements of both the phrasal verb and its object are separated. Lines 1461–3 go even further, to achieve a minor *tour de force* of syntactical dislocation, by adding the broken order of objects ('the fame . . . and the name'), the second of which is also discontinuous ('the name . . . of cruel Achilles') and stands in a chiastic relation to the first:

> That bar   up
>   *of Thebes*   *the fame*
>   upon his shuldres
>   *and the name*   *of cruel Achilles*
>   also

However, for all their structural complexity, these constructions do not operate in the service of elevated expression; the verse moves forward quickly and, as Burrow says of the poem to Book II, the diction remains simple. In his account of great poets of the ancient world Chaucer appropriately demonstrates his own skill by making departures from the common order of words seem a natural part of the essentially vigorous style of the English poetic tradition. 'In the context which this style creates,' writes Burrow, 'Dante and Thomas Chestre can exert their respective influences without coming into conflict' (1971, p. 22).

How different is the effect of similar forms of discontinuity in the Monk's laboured summary of the labours of Hercules:

> Of Hercules, the sovereyn conquerour,
> Syngen his werkes laude and heigh renoun;
> For in his tyme of strengthe he was the flour.
> He slow, and rafte the skyn of the leoun;
> He of Centauros leyde the boost adoun;
> He Arpies slow, the crueel bryddes felle;
> He golden apples rafte of the dragoun;
> He drew out Cerberus, the hounde of helle;
>
> He slow the crueel tyrant Busirus,
> And made his hors to frete hym, flessh and boon;
> He slow the firy serpent venymus;
> Of Acheloys two hornes he brak oon;
> And he slow Cacus in a cave of stoon;
> He slow the geant Antheus the stronge;
> He slow the grisly boor, and that anon;
> And bar the hevene on his nekke longe. (*MkT* 2095–2110)

38

These self-consciously elevated stanzas are far removed from the tumbling couplets of *The House of Fame*, and in their sentence-a-line construction invite comparison with the description of the tournament in *The Knight's Tale* which we have previously examined. The high style is announced in the opening lines with the inversion 'Of Hercules . . . syngen his werkes laude', where the subject is delayed and the genitive phrase qualifying it is thrown into front position. In the lines that follow, the dislocation of genitive phrases is pursued with some thoroughness: 'of strengthe . . . the flour', 'of Centauros . . . the boost', 'Of Acheloys two hornes . . . oon'. Beside these elevated dislocations there is the steady plod of 'He slow . . ., he slow . . .', so that the word-order is both more forced and more repetitive than that of *The Knight's Tale*. There is perhaps a measure of propriety in this as an expression of the Monk's grimly insistent manner in his catalogue of Fortune's victims.

Similar to the kinds of discontinuity that we have been considering are those in which a genitive phrase, or occasionally a phrase formed with another preposition, is separated from an adjective. In the following examples the discontinuity occurs in an existential clause after a front-shifted predicate adjective:

Amis 54. So mylde þey were of mood

Octavian 1455. So bryght thou art of hewe

PP B VII.99. Ac olde men and hore þat helplees ben of strengthe

CA IV.1361. This womman fair was of visage

Emaré 9. That semely ys of syght

Tr IV.736. Hire ownded heer, that sonnyssh was of hewe

LGW 1100. Ful was the feste of deyntees and rychesse

GenProl 546. Ful byg he was of brawn, and eek of bones

Thop 865. Ful strong it was of plate

MkT 2267. So ful was his corage of heigh emprise

MkT 2711. So manly was this Julius of herte

This word-order is very common in the romances, and Chaucer includes an instance in his mock-romance *Sir Thopas*. His use of it elsewhere for the purpose of emphasis is serious enough, and may be compared with the effects achieved by alternative forms of arrangement. In *Tr* IV.736, for example, he might instead have written 'that was of sonnyssh hewe', but this would weaken the force of the distinctive epithet, which, once established, can later be used less prominently: 'The myghty tresses of hire sonnysshe heeris' (IV.816). Similarly, in *GenProl* 546 either 'He was ful byg of brawn' or 'Ful byg of brawn he was' is a possible alternative, but these constructions sacrifice emphasis and phrasal balance respectively.

Occasionally a genitive phrase separated from its adjective is front-shifted:

Havelok 107. Of word, of wepne he was bold

Amis 79. Of body how wel þey were pyȝt

BD 429. Of founes, sowres, bukkes, does / Was ful the woode

But this pattern occurs more often with noun phrases. In another form of separation a comparative phrase or clause comes between an adjective and its phrasal postmodifier:

Launfal 799. Bryȝtere þan þe quene of hewe

Launfal 884. Fayryr þan þe oþer ten of syȝt

BD 994. And therto I saugh never yet a lesse / Harmful than she was in doynge

I have not found an instance of Chaucer's use of the construction with a genitive phrase. The separation in *BD* 995 suggests a limiting function as in present-day English, with the application of the comparative element 'lesse harmful' being restricted to 'doynge'; although the lady's actions were not harmful, she injured many by her beauty.

The separation of a genitive phrase from an attributive adjective by a noun is found in some ME. romances and more widely in alliterative poetry:

Havelok 180. Wis man of red, wis man of dede

Wynnere 194. Bolde sqwyeres of blode

PP B I.3. A loueli ladi of lere

PP B IX.21. a wiȝte man of strengthe

Thop 809. A perilous man of dede

In terms of modern usage this is equivalent to splitting phrases like 'a thing of great beauty' to give 'a great thing of beauty', and 'a man hard of hearing' to give 'a hard man of hearing'. The line from *Sir Thopas* appears to be the only definite instance of the construction in Chaucer's poetry, and once again may have been used in imitation of the romances. But compare *PF* 362 'The hote cormeraunt of glotenye', which if *hote* is taken in the transferred sense 'excited, eager, keen' (*OED* s.v. *hot* a. 6a) may be translated 'the cormerant, keen on gluttony'. A similar form of separation is to be seen in *MLT* 69 'The dreynte Leandre for his Erro'.

Split Genitives

The two varieties of the split genitive constitute forms of discontinuity similar to those we have been examining. One variety, comparable in structure to the asyndetic broken order of adjectives, occurs in OE. when two nouns in the genitive are separated by the noun which they jointly qualify, as in *on Herodes dagum cyninges* 'in King Herod's days'. But in late OE. the postponed noun in apposition began to drop its genitive inflexion, and this is the usual form of the construction in ME. (see

Mustanoja, pp. 78–9). A proper noun normally comes first, with a descriptive title in apposition:

Amis 321. For godes loue, heuen king
PP A V.185. And habbe Hikkes hod the ostiler
BD 142. He take up Seys body the kyng
LGW 1468. That whylom Thoas doughter was, the kyng

Notice the further separation in this last example, where the copula intervenes, and compare *HF* 391 below. The element in apposition is sometimes an epithet, as in *HF* 941 'the sonnes sone, the rede'. The reverse arrangement also occurs, with a proper noun in apposition to a descriptive title:

Orfeo A 518. For mi lordes loue, Sir Orfeo
BD 282. The kynges metynge Pharao
SqT 209. Or elles it was the Grekes hors Synon

Synon is the name of the man, not of his horse. Chaucer also uses the modern form of construction known as the group genitive; in *SqT* 672 'Til that the god Mercurius hous, the slye', for example, we find a group genitive with an epithet in apposition.

In the second and later variety of split genitive a prepositional phrase, usually one formed with *of*, comes after the noun governing the genitive:

Havelok 883. þe erles mete hauede he bouht / Of Cornwaile
Wynnere 224. for Drightyns loue in heuen
Launfal 89. To þe meyrys hous of þe toune
Launfal 278. þe kynges douȝter of Olyroun
Emaré 109. The amerayle dowghter of hethennes
CA I.1841. The kinges dowhter of Cizile
HF 391. That kynges doghtre was of Trace
Anel 52. Hath set the peples hertes bothe on fire / Of Thebes and
    Grece
Tr I.2. That was the kyng Priamus sone of Troye
SumT 1980. If it be good, in Thomas lyf of Inde
ClT 1170. For which heere, for the Wyves love of Bathe
MkT 2656. Philippes sone of Macidoyne he was
Scog 43. Scogan, that knelest at the stremes hed / Of grace, of alle
    honour and worthynesse
Malory 83/38. I am the lordis doughter of this castell

41

It will be seen that other elements in a clause may contribute to the discontinuity, most noticeably in *Havelok* 883 and *Anel* 52. The genitive phrase is sometimes transposed, as in *Emaré* 158 'Of Babylone the sowdan sonne'; but I have not noticed this form of the construction in Chaucer's poetry. The normal end position of the genitive phrase is convenient for the purpose of amplification, as in *Scog* 43–4.

It should be mentioned that the modern prepositional group genitive is first recorded in Chaucer's poetry, though it occurs under special conditions:

> *BD* 168. That was the god of slepes heyr
> *HF* 1489. The grete god of Loves name
> *Tr* I.15. For I, that God of Loves servantz serve
> *SqT* 514. Right so this god of loves ypocryte

Since in every instance we find a descriptive genitive (never a genitive of origin) governed by the noun *god*, Mustanoja's assertion that 'the present-day English type of expression, *the king of France's mother*, is first recorded in Chaucer's works' (p. 79) is not strictly accurate; Chaucer does not use the modern group genitive in comparable collocations. As G. L. Brook observes, 'the group genitive can be used only when the group of words in question is felt to be a unit with the force of a single word' (p. 151); and the evidence suggests that for Chaucer only phrases constructed with *god* had this force. The usage was rapidly extended to other nouns, so that the titles and colophon in early fifteenth-century manuscripts of *The Man of Law's Tale* include the group genitive, with the inflexion expressed by *his*, as one of three equivalent forms of construction:

> The prologe of the Mannes Tale of Lawe
> Heere begynneth the Man of Lawe his tale
> Heere endeth the tale of the Man of Lawe

Both varieties of the split genitive may be considered in relation to other forms of discontinuity and to certain types of broken order in the distribution of closely related elements on either side of a central word or group. Compare the following representative constructions used by Chaucer in his poetry:

> the kynges metynge Pharao
> her yonge suster shene
> hire streghte bak and softe
> a fair man and a boold
>
> in Thomas lyf of Inde
> that mover ys of al
> ful byg he was of brawn

Such forms of expression attest to the importance of discontinuous modification as a feature of Chaucer's syntax and style. In them we see, as Sweet suggests, 'a tendency to avoid suspensiveness' (p. 24), and also an aesthetic preference for phrasal balance.

IV CROSS ORDER

When two word-groups or sentences of similar construction follow each other, they may, in a language which has free order, be either in parallel order (anaphora) or cross order (chiasmus). Thus in Latin we have parallel order in *alio loco, alio tempore* 'in another place, at another time', cross-order in *multos defendi laesi neminem* 'I have defended many, injured none'.

Cross-order occurs in Old-English, as in *þæt land is eall weste, butan on feawun stowum styccemælum wiciaþ Finnas, on huntoþe on wintra, and on sumera on fiscoþe be þære sæ* 'the country is all desert, except that in a few places Fins dwell piecemeal, (being engaged) in hunting in winter and fishing by the sea in summer'. Here it is the result of *on sumera* being attracted by the similar group *on wintra*. This is probably the origin of the construction, although in higher stages of development it was used for emphasis and rhetorical effect. (Sweet, pp. 25–6) *vague*

It is often used to these ends in Chaucer's poetry and earlier ME. verse. While this pattern of words occurs in the Romance languages known to Chaucer, any foreign influence in particular instances would only be to strengthen a well-established native usage. This will be apparent from the range of material in the following outline, in which varieties of cross order are described with reference to the words and phrases in juxtaposition.

The cross order of attributive and predicative adjectives occurs several times in Chaucer's poetry, and numerals are juxtaposed on at least one occasion:

Arthour A 524. þe tour largge and depe þe diche

Havelok 711. Ores gode, and ful god seyl

Patience 166. Summe to Diana deuout and derf Neptune

PF 364. The throstil old; the frosty feldefare

Tr IV.1573. But lust voluptuous and coward drede

KnT 1910. Of alabastre whit and reed coral

KnT 2586. With baner whyt, and hardy chiere and face ✗ *see later comment*

MerchT 1891. Til dayes foure, or thre dayes atte leeste

PhysT 32. For right as she kan peynte a lilie whit, / And reed a rose

SecNT 225. With body cleene and with unwemmed thoght

WomNob 2. youre beaute hoole and stidefast governaunce

43

Only occasionally does zeugma occur, as in *KnT* 2586, and then probably not as a conscious trick of style; the juxtaposed adjectives are usually of the same class.

The cross order of nouns—that is, when adjectival inversion occurs in the second phrase rather than the first—is found somewhat more often:

Havelok 1761. With mikel loue and herte god

Isumbras 55. With carefull herte and sykynge sore

Launfal 382. Wyth ryche cloþes & armure bryȝt

Emaré 328. With carefulle herte and sykyng sore

Gowther 461. A reyd hors and armur bryghth

BD 1211. With sorweful herte, and woundes dede

Tr V.199. With feloun look and face dispitous

KnT 1920. The broken slepes, and the sikes colde

KnT 2134. With kempe heeris on his browes stoute

SumT 2182. As that this olde cherl with lokkes hoore

MerchT 1824. With thikke brustles of his berd unsofte

NPT 2935. For feere of blake beres, or boles blake

CYT 820. The foure spirites and the bodies sevene

MancT 258. By sadde tokenes and by wordes bolde

MancT 279. O trouble wit, o ire recchelees

There are certain points of resemblance between Chaucer and the romances in the use of this construction. In both, though it may occur in various contexts, cross order is particularly associated with the description of an unpleasant object or experience; and it will also be seen that the juxtaposed nouns often belong to a prepositional phrase introduced by with. In lines like *NPT* 2935 Chaucer reinforces the construction by alliteration; in others such as *MerchT* 1824 there is both alliteration and an emphatic rhythm.

Prepositional adjuncts sometimes occur in cross order:

GGK 1832. Gered hit watz with grene sylke and with golde schaped

LGW 2361. How she was brought from Athenes in a barge, / And in a cave how that she was brought

PrT 455. For noght oonly thy laude precious / Parfourned is by men of dignitee, / But by the mouth of children thy bountee / Parfourned is

Both of the examples from Chaucer are repetitive, for the purpose of rhetorical heightening in *PrT* 445–8 and because the juxtaposed phrases in *LGW* 2361–2 have different syntactical functions. More striking is the contrastive effect of locative adverbs in cross order:

44

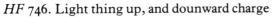

HF 746. Light thing up, and dounward charge

KnT 2755. Hym gayneth neither, for to gete his lif, / Vomyt upward, ne dounward laxatif

SqT 518. As in a toumbe is al the faire above, / And under is the corps

A genitive phrase may be found in cross order with a similar phrase or one formed with another preposition:

Havelok 1648. þicke in þe brest, of bodi long

PF 550. Most of estat, of blod the gentilleste

MillT 3337. he was somdeel squaymous / Of fartyng, and of speche daungerous

MLT 200. The strif of Thebes; and of Ercules, / Of Sampson, Turnus, and of Socrates / The deeth

MerchT 2171. First, love of Crist, and to youreself honour

Nouns qualified by genitive phrases may themselves be in cross order, as in Criseyde's rhetorical description of Troilus: 'Of trouthe grownd, mirour of goodliheed, / Of wit Apollo, stoon of sikernesse' (*Tr* II.842–3).

It remains to consider briefly the chiastic arrangement of sentence parts, beginning with subjects:

GGK 1998. Now neȝez þe Nw ȝere, and þe nyȝt passez

Tr IV.1145. and ebben gan the welle / Of hire teeris, and the herte unswelle

KnT 2743. Swelleth the brest of Arcite, and the soore / Encreesseth

In this construction the first subject and its verb are inverted, which tends to throw particular emphasis on the verbs. Finite and non-finite verbs also occur in cross order:

Havelok 235. Handes wringing, and drawing bi hor

Havelok 347. Or stede on ride, or handlen spere

Havelok 817. Wel he it bar, and solde it wel

GGK 1625. þe goude ladyez were geten, and gedered þe meyny

LGW 2085. Yow to defende, and knyghtly slen youre fo

Ven 28. Wepinge to laughe, and singe in compleynyng

Objects are more frequently met with in cross order in Chaucer's poetry, which is to say that he preferred to invert the verb and its object in the second of two co-ordinate phrases or clauses:

Havelok 2583. He brenne kirkes, and prestes binde

ABC 129. Redresse me, mooder, and me chastise

45

Tr I.688. Mistrusten alle, or elles alle leve

Tr III.25. They dreden shame, and vices they resygne

KnT 1422. Wel koude he hewen wode, and water bere

KnT 2503. Nailynge the speres, and helmes bokelynge; / Giggynge
of sheeldes, with layneres lacynge

MillT 3147. To apeyren any man, or hym defame

The cross order of subject complements is also found:

PF 2. Th'assay so hard, so sharp the conquerynge

Tr II.820. This yerd was large, and rayled alle th'aleyes

Tr V.659. The dayes moore, and lenger every nyght

Tr V.1502. And how Ypomedoun in litel stounde / Was dreynt, and
ded Parthonope of wownde

KnT 1476. The nyght was short and faste by the day

Fort 47. My lore is bet than wikke is thy grevaunce

The effect of this construction is normally to emphasise the juxtaposed
complements, as in *PF* 2, where the word-order is reinforced by
assonance. In *Tr* V.659 the juxtaposition of comparative adjectives helps
to convey a sense of time's slow passage.

Generally considered, cross order is used to achieve variety and
emphasis. The emphasis may fall on the juxtaposed words or, since
every chiasmus necessarily includes an inversion, on the words en-
closing them. Examples of both have been given, in which the effect is
often rhetorical; but to conclude here is an instance of cross order used
for a different purpose:

> Wel koude he hewen wode, and water bere,
> For he was yong and myghty for the nones,
> And therto he was long and big of bones
> To doon that any wight kan hym devyse. (*KnT* 1422–5)

The cross order of objects in line 1422 does not particularly stand out in
this description of Arcite, who has come 'disgised povrely' as a conventional hero of romance to serve in the court of Theseus. It is, in fact,
of a piece with the simple diction in briefly conjuring up the world of
popular romance, with its heroes like Havelok who are similarly 'myghty
for the nones' and 'big of bones'. These lines echo in an appropriate
context the style of *Havelok* and other romances in the English
tradition, where cross order occurs a number of times as part of the fabric
of vigorous narrative. The stylistic function of cross order on this
occasion is therefore simply its traditional propriety.

46

In careless speech it often happens that a speaker finishes a sentence grammatically, and then adds one or more words as an after-thought, to complete the meaning or define it more clearly. Such tag-sentences are frequent in Arian, so that a verb which would otherwise have end-position loses it, just as in English we may say *he came, John* instead of *he, John, came = John came*. (Sweet, p. 5)

Tag sentences are common in ME., especially if we include forms of broken order that appear to add words as an afterthought, though they are not necessarily a sign of careless speech. Under this heading we shall consider some forms of apposition and a characteristic ME. partitive expression.

Sweet's example 'He came, John' illustrates a construction that frequently occurs in Chaucer's poetry, usually with a noun phrase rather than a proper noun in apposition. The following list includes examples of objects similarly appended:

> *Havelok* 1037. Al-so þei stoden, and ofte stareden, / þe, chaum-
>   iouns, and ek the ladden
>
> *Havelok* 2499. Here him rore, þat fule file
>
> *Amis* 1506. Honourd he was, þat hende
>
> *GGK* 1729. And ȝe he lad hem bi lagmon, þe lorde and his meyny
>
> *BD* 1037. For certes she was, that swete wif, / My suffisaunce, my
>   lust, my lyf
>
> *Tr* III.1380. They wol seyn 'yis', but Lord! so that they lye, / Tho
>   besy wrecches
>
> *Tr* V.713. And thus despeired, out of alle cure, / She ladde hire lif,
>   this woful creature
>
> *LGW* 1786. There as she lay, this noble wif Lucresse
>
> *MerchT* 2257. Lo, where he sit, the lechour, in the tree
>
> *FranklT* 1240. To Britaigne tooke they the righte way, / Aurelius
>   and this magicien bisyde
>
> *ShipT* 73. And thus I lete hem ete and drynke and pleye, / This
>   marchant and this monk

Visser illustrates this form of apposition throughout the history of English and notes that in current usage it 'often has an emotional connotation, especially when the second subject is preceded by *that*' (p. 54). This remark applies to several of the examples above, in which the speaker expresses his attitude towards the subject by placing it in an emphatic position, and seems more just than Miss Schlauch's claim, in treating Chaucer's use of the construction as a colloquialism, that it demonstrates 'the impatience of a speaker who omits the subject of reference merely because it is well known to him; he hurries ahead with

47

the predication, and then, realizing the incompleteness of his statement for his listener, introduces the required noun as an appended subject (or occasionally, as object)' (p. 1107). Tag sentences of this kind are as often as not depreciatory. When the construction is used with reference to abstractions and inanimate objects rather than people, it is similarly emphatic, but tends to lack the emotional colouring:

> *Alisaunder* L 4120. Hit schal beo ful deore abouȝt / þeo tole þat was in Grece y souȝt
>
> *PP* B X.361. it shal bisitten us ful soure þe siluer þat we kepen
>
> *PF* 155. It stondeth writen in thy face, / Thyn errour
>
> *Tr* I.860. Were it for my suster, al thy sorwe
>
> Malory 28/43. hit ys in vayne thy desire

A proper noun may be in apposition to a personal pronoun from which it is separated by a verb: *Many of the examples bottom of 47*

> *Havelok* 625. He ne shal neuere, sikerlike, / Godard, wite, þat fule swike
>
> *Havelok* 2274. Hwan þat was maked, sone he sende, / Vbbe, writes fer and hende
>
> *Patience* 89. þenne he ryses radly and raykes bilyue / Jonas toward port Japh
>
> *BD* 285. He that wrot al th'avysyoun / That he mette kyng Scipioun

The construction is fairly frequent in the romances and in alliterative poetry, where one also finds the use of common nouns in apposition: *GGK* 763 'Nade he sayned hymself, segge, bot þrye'. In *LGW* 1786 Chaucer might accordingly have written 'There as she lay, Lucresse, this noble wyf', but he normally prefers the construction mentioned earlier.

A more common form of apposition in Chaucer's poetry is that in which the appended phrase consists of one or more adjectives preceded by the indefinite article:

> *Havelok* 1251. O niht saw she þer-inne a liht, / A swiþe fayr, a swiþe bryht
>
> *GenProl* 165. A Monk ther was, a fair for the maistrie
>
> *GenProl* 208. A Frere ther was, a wantowne and a merye
>
> *KnT* 1241. And art a knyght, a worthy and an able
>
> *RvT* 4165. His wyf bar hym a burdon, a ful strong

When the appended phrase contains two adjectives, it may be compared with the syndetic type of adjectival broken order (p. 32 above). In another form of attributive apposition the appended phrase contains an adjective in the superlative degree followed by a postmodifier, which is usually a relative clause:

48

Havelok 1984. And he haues on þoru his þe, / þe vn-rideste þat men
may se

Patience 437. þer he busked hym a bour, þe best þat he myʒt

PF 372. Nature held on hire hond / A formel egle, of shap the
gentilleste / That evere she among hire werkes fond

LGW 717. That other hadde a doughter, the fayreste / That tho was
in that lond estward dwellynge

MerchT 1218. I have a wyf, the worste that may be

MerchT 1713. And ful of instrumentz and of vitaille, / The mooste
deyntevous of al Ytaille

FranklT 1191. Ther saugh he hertes with hir hornes hye, / The
gretteste that evere were seyn with ye

Many other constructions in Chaucer's poetry exhibit tag order. The last
to be considered here is comparable in some respects with the common
use of a genitive phrase as a premodifier in expressions of quantity:

Launfal 479. Of Walssche knyʒtes a greet rowte

KnT 1908. That coste largely of gold a fother

MerchT 1550. And namely of wommen many a route   Front order?

Similar to this form of inversion is the tag order of partitive expressions
acting as postmodifiers:

Rom 909. But nyghtyngales, a ful gret route

BD 295. With smale foules a gret hep

SqT 382. Hire maistresse clepeth wommen a greet route

PrT 496. in which there were / Children an heep

Mustanoja (p. 84) mentions this construction briefly but does not
suggest its origin; nor does he note its use with words such as *plenty*
refering to inanimate objects:

Havelok 1729. Win hwit and red, ful god plenté

Athelston 727. Haue here besauntys good plente

MLT 443. And, sooth to seyn, vitaille greet plentee / They han hire
yeven

The construction may be seen as an inverted form of the appositive
expression of quantity in such lines as *MkT* 2434 'Is ther no morsel breed
that ye do kepe?' Tag sentences are generally less suspensive and more
concrete than those employing a genitive phrase, for in them the partitive phrase has some appositional force. Compare *Anel* 195 'And for she
yaf him daunger al his fille'.

CHAPTER III

Idiomatic Usage

Not only are conjunctions and other particles possessing little or no independent meaning the mortar of English sentences, but they may be used, especially in the spoken language, to intensify or otherwise modify the force of an expression. In this chapter we shall consider some idiomatic functions of particles, and in Chapter 4 the pleonastic use of them to repeat information conveyed by other words. It will be convenient also to include certain idiomatic features of pronominal usage under the present heading.

 OPTATIVE AND IMPERATIVE CONSTRUCTIONS

In ME. the particles *as* and *so*, from which *as* derives as a worn-down form of OE. *eall swa*, are used interchangeably as expletives in certain optative and imperative constructions. They are particularly common in asseverations of the type 'so help me God', where the particle originally had the sense of 'in that way' or 'to that extent' (*OED* s.v. *so* adv. 19):

> *GGK* 2123. As help me God and þe halydam
> *MillT* 3325. A myrie childe he was, so God me save
> *MillT* 3709. As help me God! it wol nat be 'com pa me'
> *WBProl* 605. As help me God! I was a lusty oon
> *MerchT* 2392. God helpe me so, as I am yvele apayd
> *SqT* 469. As wisly helpe me grete God of kynde

The Wife of Bath is particularly fond of asseverations with *as* (see also *WBProl* 201, 423, 596, 805). It will be noticed from these examples that optative clauses formed with *so* enjoy a greater freedom of word-order than those formed with *as*, which invariably introduces the clause and is followed by the verb. In the set expressions of colloquial usage these particles have no particular stylistic function, but elsewhere they may give an emotional tinge to a construction:

> 'Now God,' quod he, 'and alle his halwes brighte
> So wisly on my soule as have mercy,
> That of youre harm as giltelees am I
> As is Maurice my sone, so lyk youre face;
> Elles the feend me fecche out of this place!'   (*MLT* 1060–4)

The pressure of Alla's emotions is such that, in a speech consisting largely of optative clauses, he not only blends two forms of asseveration in line 1061, but also undermines the structure of the following relative clause by expressing the subject-pronoun *I*. The emotive function of *so* and *as* is also to be seen in their less frequent use in imprecations:

> *Tr* III.1387. As wolde God tho wrecches that dispise / Servise of love hadde erys also longe / As hadde Mida
>
> *Tr* III.1470. I bidde God, so yeve yow bothe sorwe

Although Kerkhof says that in Chaucer's poetry 'instances of imprecatory use with *as* do not seem to occur' (p. 35), the narrator's contemptuous dismissal of cynics in the first example provides clear evidence of this rare usage.

The use of *so* and *as* in asseverations may explain their use, by a process of extension, with verbs in the imperative mood, as Robinson (p. 679) suggests in his note to *KnT* 2302 'As keepe me fro thy vengeaunce and thyn ire'. It seems unlikely that this feature of spoken usage is due to OFr. influence, as some grammarians have claimed (see Mustanoja, p. 334). A.McI. Trounce appears to regard it as indigenous when, on the strength of a possible instance in the East Anglian romance *Sir Amadace*, he suggests that 'Chaucer may well have derived the construction from the same source as the author of *Amadace* knew' (p. 70). Although it occurs elsewhere in late ME. writings (See *MED* s.v. *also* 1d (a)), Chaucer's poetry still provides the majority of instances:

> *Tr* V.144. And, for the love of God, my lady fre, / Whomso ye hate, as beth nat wroth with me
>
> *MillT* 3776. That hoote kultour in the chymenee heere, / As lene it me, I have therwith to doone
>
> *MLT* 861. So kys hym ones in his fadres name
>
> *WBT* 1060. For Goddes love, as chees a newe requeste
>
> *FranklT* 1059. As prieth hire so greet a flood to brynge
>
> *ShipT* 242. As be to every wight buxom and meke

As Sisam observes, the construction is apparently 'a polite form in which *as, so* make the command less abrupt' (p. 37). Constance in *The Man of Law's Tale*, for example, uses it twice in succession when imploring the constable not to take her child (lines 859–61). It is also a metrical convenience equivalent to the use of the particle *ne* in negative sentences like *Lady* 63 'And therfor, swete, ne beth nat yvel apayd'.

Another remarkable idiom in Chaucer's poetry is the expletive use of *there* in optative clauses, of which only a few instances are recorded elsewhere in ME. writings:

> *ParlAges* T 664. There dere Drightyne this daye dele vs of thi blysse
>
> *Melayne* 172. Thare wery hym bothe God and sayne John
>
> *Patience* 188. þer Ragnel in his rakentes hym rere of his dremes
>
> *GGK* 838. 'Graunt mercy,' quoþ Gawayn, / 'þer Kryst hit yow forʒelde'
>
> *Tr* III.947. Ther good thrift on that wise gentil herte
>
> *Tr* III.1526. Ther God us graunte sownde and soone to mete
>
> *Tr* V.1525. 'Awey!' quod he, 'ther Joves yeve the sorwe!'
>
> *KnT* 2815. Arcite is coold, ther Mars his soule gye
>
> *FrT* 1561. 'Heyt! now,' quod he, 'ther Jhesu Crist yow blesse'
>
> *MerchT* 1307. This sentence, and an hundred thynges worse, / Writeth this man, ther God his bones corse

The construction serves to make an asseveration less abrupt in polite usage, and to intensify the force of an imprecation. Chaucer uses this idiom with some frequency in *Troilus and Criseyde* (see also II.588, III.966, 1015, V.1787–8). In Book III we find Troilus in his dawn-complaint addressing the night and the sun in the following terms:

> Thow rakle nyght, ther God, make of kynde,
> The, for thyn haste and thyn unkynde vice,
> So faste ay to oure hemysperie bynde
> That nevere more under the ground thow wynde!
>
> (1437–40)
>
> What hastow lost, why sekestow this place?
> Ther God thi light so quenche, for his grace! (1455–6)

And a little later he makes use of the expletive in an equally contemptuous imperative sentence followed, as we have seen, by an imprecation with *so*:

> What! holde youre bed ther, thow, and ek thi Morwe!
> I bidde God, so yeve yow bothe sorwe! (1469–70)

This is clearly an instance of the use of *there* 'as a brusque mode of address (often in commands) to a person or persons in the place or direction indicated; = you (that are) there' (*OED* s.v. *there* adv. 2b), which antedates the *OED*'s earliest example, from Shakespeare, by over two centuries. The usage survives in such expressions as 'Hurry up there, you'. That such constructions should first appear with any consistency in Chaucer's poetry is a measure of his commitment to representing the language of daily life.

AND

Another important particle is *and*, whose use as a co-ordinating conjunction will be described in Chapter 7; here we shall consider some of its idiomatic functions as an emphatic particle in Chaucer's poetry. *And* is found in colloquial usage from OE. onwards as a device to continue the narration 'from a previous sentence, expressed or understood' (*OED* s.v. conj. 11), and often introduces a question: 'Ða cwæð Eustachius: And ne sæde ic þ[æt] wilde deor hi gelæhton?' (*BTSuppl* s.v. conj. I). Ben Jonson in his *English Grammar* draws attention to this practice with an example from Chaucer:

> 'What?' quod she, 'and be ye wood?
> And wene ye for to doo good?' (*HF* 1713–14)

Jonson observes that '*and*, in the beginning of a sentence, serveth in stead of an Admiration [i.e. an exclamation mark]' (p. 549), and the *OED* similarly refers to its use 'in expressing surprise at, or asking truth of, what one has already heard' (s.v. conj. 12). Other examples of Chaucer's usage are:

HF 1033. 'And what sown is it lyk?' quod hee

HF 1083. And ys not this a wonder thyng?

Tr III.1474. And shal I rise, allas, and shal I so?

Tr V.1157. And Pandarus, now woltow trowen me?

LGW 2689. Allas! and shal myne hondes blody be?

CYT 1061. 'Ye,' quod the preest, 'ye, sire, and wol ye so?'

An element of surprise is clearly felt in some of these examples, which illustrate what Abbott aptly terms 'emphatic interrogation' (p. 72). The introductory particle may also be used politely to soften the force of a question; and its use by the eagle in *The House of Fame* suggests a catechismal function in keeping with his kindly yet condescending attitude as tutor to the wide-eyed Geoffrey.

And is also used for the purpose of 'emphatic assent' (Abbott, p. 72), to give a special force to promissory assertions and other declarations:

BD 1143. 'For Goddes love, telle me al.' / 'Before God,' quod he, 'and I shal'

HF 875. 'Be God,' quod he, 'and, as I leve, / Thou shalt have yet, or hit be eve, / Of every word of thys sentence / A preve by experience'

Tr V.692. Allas! and I ne may it nat amende

53

PardT 859. The pothecarie answerde, 'And thou shalt have / A thyng that . . .'

ShipT 430. 'Now wyf,' he seyde, 'and I foryeve it thee'

In imperative sentences introductory *and* may give special emphasis, or it may, on the other hand, serve to make a command seem less abrupt:

BD 555. And telleth me of youre sorwes smerte

BD 1135. And telleth me eke what ye have lore

CYT 1370. And, as ye love me, kepeth it secree

The use of this construction by the dreamer in *The Book of the Duchess* is appropriate to his rôle as the confidant of a social superior: he must not seem peremptory in his desire for information. In this respect *and* has an effect comparable to that of *as* in similar contexts; but the continuative force of *and* is also present, so that the construction helps to establish a measure of informality by implying that, because certain things are known already, there is common ground between the speakers.

Another function of *and* is to introduce explanatory and amplificatory phrases of various types. Although logically superfluous in the following sentences, it isolates and thereby emphasises an adjunct that is important to the speaker's meaning:

Tr III.318. That hem avaunte of wommen, and by name

KnT 2772. That I for yow have suffred, and so longe

Other amplificatory phrases include the adverb *namely*, which further particularises the expression:

Tr II.211. What aileth yow to be thus wery soone, / And namelich of wommen?

Tr V.1102. But often was his herte hoot and cold, / And namely that ilke nynthe nyght

ShipT 43. Free was daun John, and namely of dispence

The *OED* (s.v. *namely* adv. 1) records this as the standard form of the construction when the adverb is used in the sense 'especially'; for the non-expression of *and* compare *MLT* 312 'Of viage is ther noon eleccioun, / Namely to folk of heigh condicioun?'

An interesting use of *and* is to introduce the phrase 'God toforn'. This asseveration is first recorded in the poetry of Chaucer and Langland (see *OED* s.v. *tofore* prep. 1c), though a similar form with the preposition *before* occurs elsewhere in ME. writings. Several examples are found in *Troilus and Criseyde*, particularly in the colloquial passages of Book II:

WedGawen 638. Sir Gawen sayd, 'I wolle do more / Then for to kysse, and God before!'

Tr I.1049. And God toforn, lo, som of hem shal smerte

Tr II.992. And God toforn, I wyl be ther at pryme

Tr II.1363. And God toforn, yet shal I shape it so

Tr II.1409. In al that evere I may, and God tofore

Tr III.1639. Quod Troilus, 'I hope, and God toforn, / My deere
frend, that I shal so me beere'

This form of asseveration gives special emphasis to a resolve. Notice the
use of the two asseverations 'by God' and 'and God toforn' side by side in
Tr II.430 'By God, I shal namore come here this wyke, / And God toforn,
that am mystrusted thus'.

And has been used since OE. to introduce an amplificatory phrase in
which the demonstrative pronoun *that* refers to something in the
preceding clause, as in 'It was necessary to act, and that promptly'.
Mustanoja (p. 171) calls this the 'emphatic vicarious use' of *that*. Three
main forms of construction may be distinguished in Chaucer's poetry
according to the syntactical function of the element following the
demonstrative. *That* is most often followed by an adjunct:

Launfal 347. þey wente to bedde, & þat anoon

BD 1332. to put this sweven in ryme / As I kan best, and that anoon

Tr IV.495. How sholde I that foryete, and that so blyve?

LGW 1242. The wikke fame upros, and that anon

FrT 1592. I have been syk, and that ful many a day

MerchT 2153. And in he stirte, and that in swich manere

PardT 796. Shal renne to the town, and that ful swithe

CYProl 604. He koude werke, and that in sondry wise

MancT 303. And to the crowe he stirte, and that anon

Several instances of the construction are found in Book II of *Troilus and
Criseyde* (lines 657, 928, 1093, 1358, 1513, 1682, 1712), where it helps to
underscore the urgency with which preparations are made for the lovers'
union.

In the second form of the construction the demonstrative pronoun is
followed by a phrase referring to a noun in the preceding clause. This
phrase is occasionally nominal, as in *GenProl* 43 'A knyght ther was, and
that a worthy man', which can be seen as an expanded noun phrase in
apposition. More often we find an adjective phrase of the following type:

LGW 2327. Lo! here a dede of men, and that a ryght

GenProl 339. An housholdere, and that a greet, was he

RvT 3939. A theef he was for sothe of corn and mele, / And that a
sly

This construction is not normally used when the antecedent is premodified; a form of adjectival broken order is then preferred, as in 'a

55

good man and true' (see p. 32 above). Compare also appositive expressions like *GenProl* 208 'A Frere ther was, a wantowne and a merye' (p. 48).

Other forms of postmodification by means of an amplificatory phrase may be noted. Sometimes the phrase introduces a consecutive clause:

> *PF* 328. But foul that lyveth by sed sat on the grene, / And that so fele that wonder was to sene

> *GenProl* 343. Withoute bake mete was nevere his hous / Of fissh and flessh, and that so plentevous, / It snewed in his hous of mete and drynke

> *MillT* 3517. Shall falle a reyn, and that so wilde and wood, / That half so greet was nevere Noes flood

Or an adjective in the superlative degree may be postmodified by a phrase or a relative clause:

> *Gowther* 336. 'My lord,' he seyd, ' a mon, / And that tho feyryst that ever Y sye'

> *GenProl* 193. I seigh his sleves purfiled at the hond / With grys, and that the fyneste of a lond

Here the superl. is modified by a phrase.

Such sentences constitute an emphatic expansion of the form of apposition seen, for example, in *LGW* 717 'That other hadde a doughter, the fayreste / That tho was in that lond estward dwellynge' (p. 49 above). Similarly expanded for emphasis are expressions of quantity:

> *Gowther* 133. Bot fed hym up with rych fode / And that full mych

> *LGW* 2165. Save wilde bestes, and that ful many oon

> *PardT* 811. And heere is gold, and that ful greet plentee

In the third form of the construction the demonstrative pronoun is the subject or front-shifted object in an amplifictory clause, and it refers to a preceding imperative clause in its entirety:

> *Tr* V.1609. But beth nat wroth, and that I yow biseche

> *MillT* 3600. Go, save oure lyf, and that I the biseche

> *WBProl* 807. Foryeve it me, and that I thee biseke

> *WBProl* 853. Do, dame, telle forth youre tale, and that is best

> *MancT* 206. Foryeveth it me, and that I yow biseche

In such instances the construction is used either to suggest a measure of urgency or to soften the force of a command. The latter function is to be seen also in *WBT* 1173 'Yet may the hye God, and so hope I, / Graunte me grace to lyven vertuously', where the amplificatory clause occurs parenthetically with the adverb *so* part of an assertion. Other variations in the 'emphatic vicarious use' of *that* are no doubt to be

56

found in Chaucer's poetry, but the constructions that have been described are the most familiar. In delaying a piece of information for emphasis or some other purpose they resemble forms of tag order and broken order, and thus further attest to 'a tendency to avoid suspensiveness' in ME. syntax.

BINOMIAL VERBS

A common idiomatic function of *and* is to connect two verbs in a paratactic relationship so as to form what J. R. Firth (p. 122) calls a 'binomial'. A sentence like 'I'll go and get another one' does not represent a simple combination of 'I'll go' and 'I'll get another one'; 'go and get' is a form of hendiadys whereby the first verb, which is normally a verb of motion, loses some of its semantic identity and becomes with *and* a kind of verbal intensifier. The verbs of motion most often used in this function have been *go* since the OE. period and *come* since early ME. (see Visser, pp. 1395, 1399). In Chaucer's poetry the two verbs connected by *and* are usually in the infinitive mood, and only occasionally in the indicative:

Havelok 1660. And y ful wel rede þe / þat þou come and ete with me

Orfeo A 88. & bad hem go & hir at-hold

MillT 3620. He gooth and geteth hym a knedyng trogh

WBProl 137. To goon and usen hem in engendrure

FranklT 843. To come and romen hire in compaignye

FranklT 905. They goon and pleye hem al the longe day

PardProl 386. He wol come up and offre in Goddes name

See Kenyon (pp. 4–5) for further examples from Chaucer, and Ohlander (1936, pp. 73–86) for a discussion of ME. usage. It is often said that in a binomial construction the second verb indicates the purpose of the action specified by the verb of motion, so that 'gooth and geteth' in *MillT* 3620, for example, is equivalent to the hypotactic combination 'gooth to geten'. While this may be true in many instances, it does not account for the the form of expression in *WBProl* 137, where the verb of motion is logically superfluous. Here the hendiadys is not equivalent to 'goon to usen', but functions as a vigorous periphrasis in which the sense of motion strengthens the force of the primary verb. This is in keeping with the Wife of Bath's colloquial habits of speech, and may be compared with current usage in such sentences as 'He's just the sort of person to go and make a silly remark like that'.

Binomial verbs are more common in Chaucer's poetry when *and* is not expressed, the asyndetic form having been in frequent use since OE. with the verbs of motion *come* and *go* (see Visser, pp. 1391–7). Here first are some examples of the construction with the verbs in the infinitive:

57

Launfal 256. Bad þou schuldest com speke wyth here

WedGawen 728. We wolle go see their uprising

PP B VI.219. And ʒif the gomes grucche bidde hem go swynke

Tr II.1171. 'Now, em,' quod she, 'we wol go dyne anon'

MillT 3685. Therfore I wol go slepe an houre or tweye

RvT 4250. I wol go crepen in by my felawe

WBProl 108. Bad nat every wight he sholde go selle / Al that he
hadde

SumT 2241. Now ete youre mete, and lat the cherl go pleye; / Lat
hym go honge hymself a devel weye

FranklT 1334. And if ye vouche sauf, ye may go see

MancT 169. Yet hath this brid, by twenty thousand foold, / Levere
in a forest, that is rude and coold, / Goon ete wormes and swich
wrecchednesse

The asyndetic construction more clearly illustrates the idiomatic
character of binomial verbs. In most of these examples the expression of
purpose is very weak, especially when the verb of motion is *go*; this verb
is used periphrastically to lend emphasis to the primary verb. Kenyon (p.
5) draws attention to the colloquial nature of the construction and to its
often derogatory connotation in passages of dialogue in Chaucer's
poetry. The following examples capture something of the Wife of Bath's
contempt for demanding husbands, and it is possible that they illustrate
a different relationship between the two verbs:

WBProl 653. Man shal nat suffre his wyf go roule aboute

WBProl 657. And suffreth his wyf to go seken halwes

Kenyon (p. 6) suggests that here the second infinitive expresses manner
rather than purpose—that is, 'to go gadding about' in line 653—and that
the construction is therefore comparable to the use of *come* with an
infinitive of manner, as in *Tr* II.1253 'ysee who comth here ride'. But
Mustanoja (p. 537) is sceptical, and notes that the use of *go* with an
infinitive of manner is not attested elsewhere in ME. writings.

Asyndetic binomial verbs are sometimes found in the imperative
plural in Chaucer's poetry:

CMundi T 14688. Goþ lokeþ þe sawes of ʒoure lay

MkT 2194. 'Gooth bryngeth forth the vesseles,' quod he

CYT 1207. Gooth walketh forth and brynge us a chalk stoon

The entire phrase 'gooth walketh forth' in the last example seems to
stand in a paratactic relation to the verb *brynge*; the periphrasis suggests
a measure of pomposity affected by the canon in an attempt to win the
confidence of his victim. It is more usual to find the verbs in the imperative singular:

Amis 524. & go play þe in to þe gardin

Gowther 232. Go schryfe the, modur, and do tho best

Gowther 338. Cum loke on hym, it is no lye

Amadace 214. Go loke thou dighte oure soper syne

BD 749. 'Blythely,' quod he; 'com sytte adoun'

HF 1790. Goo blowe this folk a sory grace

Tr II.396. And therfore, er that age the devoure, / Go love

KnT 2760. Fare wel phisik! go ber the man to chirche

MillT 3600. Go save oure lyf, and that I the biseche

SumT 2026. Go lede hym to the deeth, I charge thee

PhysT 201. Go bryng hire forth, and put hire in oure warde

Although it is not always possible to tell from the form of the second verb whether in the singular it is an imperative or an infinitive, the plural usage suggests that 'originally the two constituents were both imperative forms' (Visser, p. 1398). This does not mean, however, that the construction is to be treated disjunctively, as editors tend to do by inserting a comma between the two verbs. For one thing, *go* and *come* are always lightly stressed in this function in verse. There are also constructions like that in *Amis* 524, where the adjunct 'in to þe gardin' applies to the verb of motion only and the second verb must therefore be an infinitive.

One last form of binomial construction remains to be mentioned. This occurs when *go* is used in the hortatory subjunctive mood and is separated from an infinitive of purpose by the subject-pronoun *we*:

Tr II.615. A, go we se! cast up the yates wyde

Tr II.1163. Therwith she lough, and seyde, 'Go we dyne'

Tr V.523. As go we sen the palais of Criseyde

FranklT 1217. 'Go we thanne soupe,' quod he, 'as for the beste'

ShipT 223. What! lat us heere a messe, and go we dyne

 IV   *IT* AS AN INDEFINITE OBJECT

Mustanoja (p. 134) in his brief notice of the neuter pronoun *it* as an anticipatory object cites the following examples:

HarlLyr 32.1. Lutel wot hit any mon / hou derne loue may stonde

RvT 3980. And straunge he made it of hir mariage

There is, however, a significant difference between these sentences. In the first the proleptic pronoun can be omitted without disturbing its structure and meaning; but the same pronoun cannot be omitted in the second sentence, because 'made it straunge' forms a unit in which *it* is used idiomatically without reference to the following phrase. The construction survives in such expressions as 'play it safe'. For a full outline of this usage, which has taken various forms in the history of English, see Visser (pp. 449–57). The varieties there recorded, such as 'lord it', 'rough it', 'make it out', and others now obsolete, answer to a need felt by generations of speakers for concise and graphic idioms, and in them the particles are used symbolically.

In Chaucer's poetry the idiom most often occurs with the verb *make*, which derives from OE. *hit macian* 'to act, behave', as in 'Swa swa he hit macode on his life' (*BTSuppl* s.v. *macian* VI 1). In ME. this phrase normally takes an adjective specifying the kind of behaviour; and the frequency with which adjectives like *quaint, strange,* and *tough* occur suggests that the idiom was particularly associated with difficult behaviour:

> *CA* I.283. It nedeth noght to make it queinte
>
> *BD* 531. He made hyt nouther towgh ne queynte
>
> *Tr* V.101. If that I speke of love, or make it tough
>
> *GenProl* 785. Us thoughte it was noght worth to make it wys
>
> *FranklT* 1223. He made it straunge, and swoor, so God hym save
>
> *ShipT* 379. And up he gooth and maketh it ful tough

The precise sense in which the idiom is used varies according to the context; in the last example, as Elliott notes, 'the meaning is plainly bawdy' (p. 95). John Palsgrave writing in the early sixteenth century has some interesting notes on the construction in his *Lesclarcissement de la langue françoyse*:

> I make it coye, or nyes, as a daungerouse person doth. *Je fais lestrange*. Whye make you it so coye, thynke you men knowe you nat: *pour quoy fayctez vous lestrange ainsi, pencés vous quon ne vous congnoysse poynt.*
>
> I make it tough, I make it coye, as maydens do, or persons that be strange if they be asked a questyon. *Je fais le dangereux, je me fais prier.* Mary, you make it toughe: *Marie, vous faitez le dangereux.* (p. 624)

Palsgrave's brief explanations suggest something of the force of the idiom in Chaucer's poetry, and his examples of French usage illustrate a comparable construction that possibly reinforced the native expression in the late ME. period. In the course of the sixteenth century certain phrases of this type were effectively compressed by converting the adjective into a verb; 'to make it coy', for example, was replaced by 'to coy it'. Shakespeare uses the older idiom with *make* once or twice, but it appears to have died out in the seventeenth century. The resemblance to a similar construction in a sentence from a recent novel quoted by Visser (p. 452), 'You don't have to tell me he's made it tough for you', is purely formal; the phrase 'made it tough' is here equivalent to 'made matters difficult', not 'behaved in a difficult manner'.

It is seldom used as an indefinite object with other verbs in Chaucer's poetry. The colloquial expression 'to have it hot', which has no early parallels, occurs twice in *Troilus and Criseyde* in the sense 'to be passionately in love', and is comparable in form and meaning to the transatlantic idiom 'He's got it bad'. It is used first by Troilus and later by Pandarus:

> *Tr* III.1650. I hadde it nevere half so hote as now
>
> *Tr* IV.583. but hadde ich it so hoote, / And thyn estat, she sholde go with me

This construction conforms to the standard ME. pattern verb + *it* + adjective. Examples of the later pattern verb + *it*, common in Elizabethan English, cannot be established with certainty:

> *HF* 1119. And though to clymbe hit greved me
>
> *MerchT* 2273. Yit shul we wommen visage it hardily

Neither of these examples has parallels in ME. Skeat says of the construction in *HF* 1119: '"To climbe hit", i.e. to climb the rock; still a common idiom' (vol. 3, p. xv). But *hit* may take *roche* in line 1116 as its antecedent, or be pleonastic after the infinitive subject 'to clymbe'. The use of *it* in *MerchT* 2273 might similarly be explained as being to provide the object of the nonce-verb *visage* in the sense 'to face, confront' (*OED* s.v. I) or 'put a bold face on' (*Glossary* s.v.), though in either case the meaning of the pronoun is vague, and there is just a possibility that 'visage it' is an idiomatic combination indicating behaviour of the kind described in the next line ('And wepe, and swere, and chyde subtilly'). This example illustrates what is often a fine line between idiomatic and non-idiomatic functions of *it* as an object-pronoun in the history of English.

 PERSONAL REFERENCE

The final aspect of idiomatic expression to be considered in this chapter is the use of personal pronouns and demonstrative adjectives in noun phrases referring to people. The specification of a noun by a personal pronoun in the first or second person plural, a construction in which the pronoun has the force of a demonstrative, is found in all periods of the language and occasionally in Chaucer's poetry:

> *Tr* III.772. So as ye wommen demen alle
>
> *SumT* 1883. The clennesse and the fastynge of us freres
>
> *SumT* 1912. I speke of us, we mendynantz, we freres

MerchT 2273. Yit shul we wommen visage it hardily

PrT 688. Preye eek for us, we synful folk unstable.

The construction enables the speaker to identify himself or his listener(s) as belonging to a particular group, but it tends also to have an emotive force that registers his attitude towards the group. The phrase 'ye wommen' used by Pandarus to Criseyde in *Tr* III.772 has a patronising, derogatory connotation comparable to that in modern usage ('You academics are all the same'). In the first person, on the other hand, the construction promotes a sense of attachment rather than detachment and can suggest a certain self-consciousness and pride, as in the friar's usage in *The Summoner's Tale*. The switch from *us* to *we* in his second sentence and in *PrT* 688 shows that for Chaucer the subjective was the stronger form, whereas in modern colloquial and dialectal speech ('We're busy men, us farmers') the opposite is the case (see *OED* s.v. *us* 5b).

A peculiarity of Early English syntax is the demonstrative use of third person singular pronouns with proper nouns (see Mustanoja, pp. 135–6), which occurs with some frequency in Chaucer's poetry:

HF 405. How fals eke was he Theseus

Tr I.786. As sharp as doth he Ticius in helle

Tr V.212. In furie, as doth he Ixion in helle

LGW 1544. Bytwixe hym Jason and this Ercules

KnT 1210. Bitwixen Theseus and hym Arcite

MLT 940. To sleen hym Olofernus in his tente

WBProl 498. As was the sepulcre of hym Daryus

WBProl 643. How he Symplicius Gallus lefte his wyf

MerchT 1294. Of whiche he Theofraste is oon of tho

MerchT 1368. And slow hym Olofernus, whil he slepte

MerchT 1373. and made hym Mardochee / Of Assuere enhaunced for to be

SqT 250. Save that he Moyses and kyng Salamon

MkT 2673. Up roos he Julius, the conquerour

NPT 3394. Certes, he Jakke Straw and his meynee

Visser's examples of this construction (p. 53) are mainly from late OE. prose, though it is recorded in Laȝamon's *Brut* and at least as late as Lydgate (see Courmont, pp. 67–8). A typical use is in the citation of *exempla* and authorities, which suggests that it belonged to literary rather than colloquial style and may account for its absence from the romances. The demonstrative force of the pronoun helps to draw attention to the person named and can imply a measure of familiarity; but familiarity breeds contempt, and it is noticeable that Chaucer quite often uses the construction in a depreciatory context. The Merchant in his ironic celebration of the wedding of January and May refers dis-

The romances are then colloquial style,

paragingly to 'he Theodamus' (*MerchT* 1720), whose trumpet at Thebes sounded not half so clearly as the minstrelsy at the feast, and then moves on to belittle the efforts of the poet Martianus Capella, whom he addresses familiarly with the singular pronoun *thou*:

> Hoold thou thy pees, thou poete Marcian,
> That writest us that ilke weddyng murie
> Of hire Philologie and hym Mercurie,
> And of the songes that the Muses songe!
> To smal is bothe thy penne, and eek thy tonge,
> For to descryven of this mariage.   (*MerchT* 1732–7)

The reference to 'hire Philologie and hym Mercurie' is of a piece with the narrator's ironic contempt for the poet himself as part of a common rhetorical topos. Since the person named is usually an authority or worthy of the past, the demonstrative use in *NPT* 3394 to specify a leader of the Peasant's Revolt is clearly humorous. The construction occurs less often, and therefore with particular emphasis, when the reference is to a character in the narrative itself, as in *LGW* 1544 'hym Jason' and *KnT* 1210 'hym Arcite'. It is possibly an indication of the narrator's sympathies in *The Knight's Tale* that Arcite rather than Palamon should be treated in this way.

ME. poets commonly use the demonstrative adjective *this* in referring to their characters, a narrative device which generally suggests a measure of both informality and familiarity:

> Now this gome alle in grene so gayly attyrede,
> This hathelle one this heghe horse with hauke one his fiste,
> He was ȝonge and ȝape and ȝernynge to armes.
>
> (*ParlAges* 169–71)

Present-day anecdotal practice ('This fellow comes up to me and says . . .') is rather different, since the demonstrative is normally used only for the first mention of an item. As Cornelius Novelli remarks, Chaucer 'seldom uses the demonstrative adjective to refer to a person unless the person has been at least somewhat characterized' (p. 247). Novelli discusses various literary functions of *this*, such as its use as a device of characterisation:

> When characters have certain inexpressible but unmistakable qaulities Chaucer tends, especially with the comic characters, to let the name carry its own associations, the demonstrative adjective appealing to the reader's own perception of the character. What, for example, could sum up the totality of Chauntecleer better than the repeated 'this Chauntecleer'? (pp. 247–8)

But perhaps more significant is his observation that

> at the same time that the demonstrative adjective draws the reader's attention into the story, as a colloquial device it reminds him that

someone is telling the story, controlling the total effect. And insofar as the narrator controls the materials of his story, he is at a certain artistic distance from them. (p. 248)

That is to say, the demonstrative may be used to convey the narrator's attitude towards his material; depending on the context, it can suggest either engagement with or detachment from the subject. In *The Knight's Tale*, for example, the emotive repetition of the demonstrative in such lines as 'This Theseus, this duc, this worthy knyght' (2190) would seem to reflect the Knight's respect for Theseus; and it is of interest that in this tale instances of 'this Palamon' outnumber those of 'this Arcite' by about three to one. In other contexts the effect of *this* may be depreciatory: for example, with reference to unfaithful lovers like 'this fals Arcite' (*Anel* 141) and 'this Eneas' (*LGW* 1285). In *LGW* 1544 'Bytwixe hym Jason and this Ercules' the narrator registers his disapproval by using two forms of pejorative reference. Although it is perhaps impossible to generalise about such a common feature of Chaucer's narrative, the emotive functions of *this* deserve closer study.

It is easier to see a pattern in Chaucer's use of the plural demonstrative *these*, one of whose functions is to refer 'to things or persons familiarly known, esp. to the whole class of such things or persons' (*OED* s.v. II 1c). In this respect it can be considered the third person equivalent of generalising constructions with personal pronouns ('we freres', 'ye wommen'):

> *MerchT* 1889. As custume is unto thise nobles alle
>
> *FranklT* 818. As doon thise noble wyves whan hem liketh
>
> *PardT* 538. Thise cookes, how they stampe, and streyne, and grynde
>
> *CYT* 1397. They mowe wel chiteren as doon thise jayes

In ME. as in modern usage ('Who do these Russians think they are?') the familiarity often has an edge to it, notably in references to lovers in Chaucer's poetry:

> *Tr* I.926. Thise loveres wolden speke in general
>
> *Tr* II.1306. That lay, as do thise lovers in a traunce
>
> *LGW* 1167. As don these lovers, as I have herd seyd
>
> *KnT* 1531. As doon thise loveres in hir queynte geres

Another use of *these* is in reference to the authority of old books and people:

> *Tr* V.1753. As men may in thise olde bokes rede
>
> *LGW* F 19. And to the doctrine of these olde wyse
>
> *LGW* F 575. After thise olde auctours lysten for to trete
>
> *WBT* 1004. 'Thise olde folk kan muchel thyng,' quod she

FranklT 709. Thise olde gentil Britouns in hir dayes / Of diverse
      aventures maden layes

For this use without *old* compare *MkT* 2121 'as thise clerkes maken
mencioun' and *Buk* 20 'as seyn these wise'. Here again the demonstrative may add a subjective touch, with familiarity shading into superi-
ority; there is, for example, a slightly patronising note in the Franklin's
use of the construction. Although we may never recover the full significance of these and other forms of idiomatic usage in medieval poetry,
they offer a wide and interesting field for investigation beyond the
familiar territory occupied by *you* and *thou* as polite and impolite forms
of address.

CHAPTER IV

Pleonasm

Particles are often used pleonastically in Chaucer's poetry to reinforce the structure of sentences and to secure special effects. In this chapter we shall consider the iterative functions of personal and demonstrative pronouns and, more briefly, of conjunctions and prepositions. Reference will also be made to some forms of clausal extraposition so as to illustrate the anticipatory use of certain pronouns. Many of the constructions to be described are still found in colloquial speech and writing, but it does not follow that their use by Chaucer and his contemporaries was similarly restricted to informal style.

I SUBJECT-PRONOUNS

The repetition of a phrasal or clausal subject by means of a personal or demonstrative pronoun later in the sentence occurs throughout the history of English (see Visser, pp. 56–7) and is extremely common in ME. poetry. A rough distinction can be made between close (or emphatic) repetition, when a pleonastic pronoun directly follows the subject or is separated from it by only a few words, and distant (or structural) repetition, when a pleonastic pronoun is separated from the subject by a longer sequence of words. Miss Schlauch (p. 1104) distinguishes between colloquial and literary forms of repetition on similar grounds, but this does not altogether accord with the facts of Chaucer's usage; context is a more important factor than length of separation in determining the level of style. For the purpose of this outline, a repetition will be considered distant when it extends beyond three lines of verse.

We shall begin with repetitions that occur within a single line of verse. In the purest form of close repetition there is contact between a noun phrase and a pleonastic subject-pronoun, as in 'The bells they sound so clear' (A. E. Housman). This construction, now considered a colloquialism in ordinary usage and an archaic feature of the ballad style in verse, is found in all periods of the language and regularly occurs in some of the ME. rhyming romances. Besides its usefulness as a metrical expedient, it is often emphatic and 'may give a picturesque or graphic touch to a sentence' (Onions, p. 133):

Amis 169. þat riche douke, he loued hem so

Amis 264. Mine hert, it brekeþ of þre

Athelston 51. Hys name it was Alryke

Launfal 386. Gyfre, he rood all behynde

BD 1240. Trewly hir answere hyt was this

Tr IV.209. But Antenor, he shal com hom to towne

WBT 1191. Verray poverte, it syngeth proprely

MerchT 2087. Which jalousye it was so outrageous

PardT 776. The worste of hem, he spak the firṣte word

Thop 901. But sir Thopas, he bereth the flour / Of roial chivalry

In the last example Chaucer is faithful to the style of the romances; but this form of pleonasm is also fairly common elsewhere in his poetry. The construction is often forceful in its effect by allowing for a slight pause after the subject before the sentence is resumed; it has in fact been described as a form of 'anticipatory substitution', whereby a noun phrase in front position is 'marked off by intonation or punctuation from what follows' (Quirk and Greenbaum, p. 280). This is the converse of the form of apposition in such sentences as *PF* 155 'It stondeth writen in thy face, / Thyn errour', where the pronoun anticipates a noun phrase in tag order (see p. 48 above). The degree of emphasis achieved by pronominal repetition partly depends on the context in which it occurs. In *Athelston* 51 the effect of the construction is negligible, because the sense of the line, as often in the romances, does not call for emphatic treatment.

There may also be contact repetition when the subject is a noun clause:

Launfal 688. þat þou lyuest, hyt ys pyté

SqT 579. Wher me was wo, that is no questioun

Repetition is particularly common after an infinitive noun clause: *Any substantiation?*

Havelok 802. To liggen at hom it is ful strong

WedGawen 668. To chese the best itt is froward

Tr III.583. Although with hym to gon it was no fere

Tr IV.959. Thus to ben lorn, it is my destinee

MerchT 1268. To take a wyf it is a glorious thyng

ShipT 290. But goldlees for to be, it is no game

Compare the converse arrangement in sentences having an anticipatory subject-pronoun with an infinitive clause in end position (p. 80 below).

Sometimes within a single line of verse the pleonastic pronoun follows a relative clause qualifying a nominal or pronominal subject:

HSynne 9165. But þat þey wroght, hyt was yn veyn

Anel 112. That al that lyked hym hit dyde her ese

FranklT 720. Thyng that I speke, it moot be bare and pleyn

There is an effect of parallelism when the pleonastic pronoun is identical in form with the subject, as in *MerchT* 2410 'He that mysconceyveth, he mysdemeth'. More often the repetition occurs after the intervention of some form of adjunct:

Isumbras 418. Thenne syr Isumbras thydur he thoghte

RelLyr XIV 106.15. þe Ryuers in-to þe see þei renne

PP B VIII.112. Thouȝte and I thus thre days we ȝeden

KnT 2868. His officers with swifte feet they renne

MillT 3649. And Alisoun ful softe adoun she spedde

RvT 3857. Diverse folk diversely they seyde

SqT 202. Diverse folk diversely they demed

As well as contributing to rhythmic effects, pleonasm tends to emphasise the connexion between the actor previously specified and the action itself. In the case of adjuncts which collocate with verbs of motion the construction may help to convey an impression of speed. A rather different effect is achieved in *RvT* 3857 and *SqT* 202, which capture a sense of animated conversation more forcibly than *MLT* 211 'Diverse men diverse thynges seyden'. In these and similar instances of close repetition it would seem that the pleonastic pronoun functions as a kind of verbal intensifier.

The construction frequently occurs within two lines of verse, with the pleonastic pronoun coming at the beginning of the second line. Here first are some examples of contact repetition when the subject is a noun phrase:

Launfal 499. And euery day, Dame Triamour, / Sche com to Syr Launfal bour

Emaré 994. And other lordys of gret valowre / They also kessed Segramowre

Tr II.979. lo, myn herte, / It spredeth so for joie

KnT 2131. The cercles of his eyen in heed, / They gloweden bitwixen yelow and reed

MillT 3167. but this Millere / He nolde his wordes for no man forbere

Thop 742. Ful many a mayde, bright in bour, / They moorne for hym paramour

Separation may be caused by various elements, such as an adjunct, a subordinate clause, or a parenthetic clause:

> *Amis* 1213. þat riche douke, wiþ wreþe & wrake, / He bad men schuld þo leuedis take
>
> *Athelston* 297. But ȝit the qwene, as ȝe schole here, / Sche callyd vpon a messangere
>
> *Tr* II.208. And with that word tho Pandarus, as blyve, / He took his leve
>
> *Tr* V.74. And Troilus, al nere his herte light, / He peyned hym with al his fulle myght
>
> *MerchT* 1423. And eek thise olde wydwes, God it woot, / They konne so muchel craft on Wades boot

A relative clause referring to the headword in a noun phrase frequently comes between it and a pleonastic subject-pronoun:

> *Havelok* 481. But þe knaue, þat litel was, / He knelede bifore þat Iudas
>
> *Emaré* 217. Then the lordes that wer grete, / They wesh and seten don to mete
>
> *Tr* IV.685. Thise wommen, which that in the cite dwelle, / They sette hem down
>
> *RvT* 4168. Aleyn the clerk, that herde this melodye, / He poked John
>
> *SqT* 181. The hors of bras, that may nat be remewed, / It stant as it were to the ground yglewed

The iteration of a subject-pronoun after a relative clause contributes to a strong emotional effect in the following lines from Thisbe's complaint:

> And now, ye wrechede jelos fadres oure,
> We that whilom were children youre,
> We preyen yow, withouten more envye,
> That in o grave yfere we moten lye.   (*LGW* 900–3)

Here the pleonasm is found beside a form of possessive postmodification ('fadres oure', 'children youre') that is not attested elsewhere in Chaucer's works; the resulting emphasis on pronominal forms gives a special intensity to Thisbe's condemnation of parental interference. Pleonastic constructions of this kind are generally less emphatic when, as is often the case, the repetition comes later in the second line:

> *Emaré* 52. The emperes, that fayr ladye, / Fro her lord gan she dye
>
> *HF* 1386. Her heer, that oundy was and crips, / As burned gold hyt shoon to see

MerchT 1366. Lo Judith, as the storie eek telle kan, / By wys conseil she Goddes peple kepte

The forms of pleonasm described so far often lend emphasis to the verb in passages of narrative and to the subject in passages of description, according to the length and nature of the separation. When the construction extends to three lines of verse, it allows for a further measure of amplification of the subject, and the pleonastic pronoun may come with particular force:

Amis 1075. Ac þe steward ful of envie, / Wiþ gile & wiþ trecherie, / He haþ me wrouȝt swiche sorn

HSynne 9138. þese men þat ȝede so karolland, / Alle þat ȝere hand yn hand, / þey neuer oute of þat stede ȝede

ParlAges 169. Now this gome alle in grene so gayly attyrede, / This hathelle one this heghe horse with hauke one his fiste, / He was ȝonge and ȝape and ȝernynge to armes

BD 620. The trayteresse fals and ful of gyle, / That al behoteth, and nothyng halt, / She goth upryght and yet she halt

Tr V.1723. This Pandarus, that al thise thynges herde, / And wiste wel he seyde a soth of this, / He nought a word ayeyn to hym answerde

MkT 2023. Sampsoun, this noble almyghty champioun, / Withouten wepen, save his handes tweye, / He slow and al torente the leoun

Obviously, the longer the line of verse, the greater the opportunity for elaboration and the more emphatic the repetition. The special character of the pleonasm in certain of these examples may be gauged by comparison with the use of repetition later in the third line:

KnT 2450. Saturne anon, to stynten strif and drede, / Al be it that it is agayn his kynde, / Of al this strif he gan remedie fynde

Here the pleonastic pronoun passes unnoticed; our attention is being drawn to the strife rather than to Saturn himself.

Pleonastic constructions extending beyond three lines of verse constitute forms of distant repetition. While they may still be emphatic, they are more generally used to reinforce the structure of a sentence after a delay:

Arthour L 637. Anon þeo feond þat y of tolde / þat wonede in þe eyr so bolde / And tempted so þat gode womman, / Into þeo eorþe he lyȝhte þan

Tr V.435. This Sarpedoun, as he that honourable / Was evere his lyve, and ful of heigh largesse, / With al that myghte yserved ben on table, / That deynte was, al coste it gret richesse, / He fedde hem day by day

While distant repetition occurs only occasionally in the romances, there are many examples in Chaucer's poetry, especially in *Troilus and Criseyde* (see *PF* 393–9, *Tr* I. 106–10, II.449–55. III.981–7, V.281–6, 1464–8, *KnT* 1035–41). Chaucer's pleonastic constructions seldom extend beyond seven lines, which in his rhyme royal verse is a practical limit set by the length of the stanza. He could, of course, sustain a nominal construction for the length of a stanza without repetition (compare *Tr* III.512–18, IV.806–12).

Certain forms of pleonastic construction may now be considered irrespective of the distance between the subject and a pleonastic pronoun. When the subject is a noun clause introduced by a generalising pronoun or adjective, it is often in ME. repeated pronominally before the verb:

Amis 2483. Who þerof rouȝt, he was a queede

GGK 1849. Bot who-so knew þe costes þat knit are þerinne, / He wolde hit prayse at more prys

HF 447. Which whoso willeth for to knowe, / He moste rede many a rowe / On Virgile

PF 46. And seyde hym what man, lered other lewed, / That lovede commune profyt, wel ithewed, / He shulde into a blysful place wende

LGW 1614. For whoso wol this aventure acheve, / He may nat wel asterten

SecNT 288. Whoso that troweth nat this, a beest he is

For non-repetition of the subject compare *BD* 32 'who aske this / Leseth his asking trewely'. The word-order in some sentences necessitates repetition: for example, after extraposition of the subject for emphasis in exclamations:

Tr III.804. Allas! conceytes wrong, / What harm they don

KnT 1785. The god of love, a, *benedicite!* / How myghty and how greet a lord is he

PardT 538. Thise cookes, how they stampe, and streyne, and grynde

Similarly, there is emphatic extraposition and repetition of the subject in certain interrogative constructions:

WBProl 72. Virginitee, thanne wherof sholde it growe?

MerchT 2412. This Januarie, who is glad but he?

CYT 1341. This sotted preest, who was gladder than he?

Visser (p. 55) notes that this construction is first found in ME., and compares the French 'Votre père est-il malade?' It will be seen to serve a rhetorical function in the first example, and in the others to convey an impression of innocence.

When the subject of a sentence is followed by a temporal clause, it is often repeated pronominally before the postponed verb:

> *Octavian* 460. The lyenas, thorow Goddys grace, / When sche sye the ladyes face, / Debonerly stylle sche stode

> *GGK* 1623. þe lorde ful lowde with lote and laȝter myry, / When he seȝe Sir Gawayn, with solace he spekez

> *Tr* V.57. Criseyde, whan she redy was to ride, / Ful sorwfully she sighte

> *KnT* 1123. This Palamon, whan he tho wordes herde, / Dispitously he looked and answerde

> *WBProl* 64. Th'apostel, whan he speketh of maydenhede, / He seyde that precept therof hadde he noon

> *WBT* 1193. The povre man, whan he goth by the weye, / Before the theves he may synge and pleye

> *MkT* 2351. Aurelian, whan that the governaunce / Of Rome cam into his handes tweye, / He shoop upon this queene to doon vengeaunce

A similar sentence-pattern with repetition occurs in OFr.: 'li borgois de Troies, quant il virent le desastre, il furent molt esbabi'. The subject of the temporal clause is normally identical with that of the principal clause. For an instance of non-repetition compare *KnT* 1596–8.

When a temporal clause intervenes between the subject and predicate, the sentence is sometimes anacoluthic:

> *KnT* 2987. The Firste Moevere of the cause above, / Whan he first made the faire cheyne of love, / Greet was th'effect, and heigh was his entente

> *SumT* 1700. This frere, whan he looked hadde his fille / Upon the tormentz of this sory place, / His spirit God restored, of his grace

The form of *nominativus pendens* in these instances (for another form see p. 76 below) may be described as the extraposition of the logical subject of the temporal clause for emphasis; and it is noticeable that in both sentences there is, moreover, emphatic inversion in the predicate. Chaucer sacrifices logic to emphasis for a purpose. In *KnT* 2987–9 the construction is appropriate in its suspensiveness to Theseus' high theme, though some might wish to see in it a flicker of the uncertainty that eventually brings his grand Boethian argument to a firmly pagan conclusion. In *SumT* 1700–2 the extraposition gives a graphic touch to the description of the friar as he contemplates the torments of hell, momentarily suspended like the construction itself; the unexpected change of subject, after a further measure of delay caused by front-shifting of the object 'his spirit', then comes as a fitting expression of God's power. This little scene would be less vivid had Chaucer employed the more logical construction 'Whan that this frere looked hadde his fille'.

72

When the object of a verb or preposition is front-shifted for emphasis, it has been a common practice since OE. to repeat it later in the sentence in the form of a personal or demonstrative pronoun (see Visser, pp. 518–21). This usage is now considered colloquial, but it had a literary standing in earlier periods of English. Ben Jonson in his *English Grammar* observes that 'superfluity also of Nounes is much used' (p. 532) and gives an example from Chaucer:

> For swich lawe as a man yeveth another wight,
> He sholde hymselven usen it, by right.   (*MLT* 43–4)

Apart from being a metrical convenience, the pleonastic pronoun helps to balance the structure of this sentence by clarifying the relation of the object to both verbs, *yeveth* and *usen*. Although the repetition may now seem illogical, in such sentences it completes the expression and can hardly be considered a sign of unselfconscious speech.

Repetition of the object differs from that of the subject in certain obvious ways. While the pleonastic pronoun may on occasion be emphatic, it normally has a structural function, with the emphasis falling on the front-shifted object itself. It is also clear that, since the usual place of the object-pronoun is after a verb, there is less opportunity for contact repetition; where this does occur, it thus has a particular force. Another feature of this form of extraposition that may be used to advantage is the initial ambiguity of the front-shifted element, which, unless it is a pronoun, does not formally indicate its syntactical function. As a result the construction can sometimes give an impression of anacoluthon, as if the element in front position were an abandoned subject.

As with pleonastic expression of the subject, repetition of the object is sometimes a necessary consequence of extraposition. In *LGW* F 256 'Thy faire body, lat yt nat appere' and similar imperative sentences the object-pronoun is obligatory; but it has not seemed essential to make this distinction in the following lists of examples. Here first are instances of close repetition within a single line of verse:

Gowther 191. Yong and old, he con hom greve

WedGawen 71. And that is amys I shalle amend itt

PP B V.292. For-thi haue mercy in this mynde and marchandise, leue it

BD 691. For nothyng I leve hyt noght

TR III.402. And this that thow doost, calle it gentilesse

Tr III.1769. And hertes colde, hem wolde I that he twiste

MancT 81. That that I spak, I seyde it in my bourde

In allowing for a pause after the front-shifted object, the construction may be used to give special prominence to an idea, and, as in the line

73

from *Piers Plowman*, to suggest the meaning 'so far as that is concerned'. Contact between the two forms of the object is occasionally found when the order of subject and verb is inverted, and gives point to Troilus' denunciation of hard-heartedness in *Tr* III.1769.

The pleonastic construction more frequently extends to two lines of verse:

> *Havelok* 2624. þe firste kniht þat he þer mette, / Wiþ þe swerd so he him grette
>
> *HSynne* 9124. þe nexte day þe arme of Aue / He fonde hyt lyggyng aboue the graue
>
> *Isumbras* 22. His gentylnesse nor his curtesye / There kowthe no man hit discrye
>
> *Tr* II.1180. But Pandarus, that in a studye stood, / Er he was war, she took hym by the hood
>
> *Tr* III.416. this grete emprise / Perfourme it out
>
> *LGW* 2363. And al the tyng that Tereus hath wrought, / She waf it wel
>
> *MillT* 3776. That hoote kultour in the chymenee heere, / As lene it me
>
> *MerchT* 2051. And thynges whiche that were nat doon abedde, / He in the gardyn parfourned hem and spedde
>
> *FranklT* 1228. This wyde world, which that men seye is round, / I wolde it yeve

The occasionally anacoluthic effect of the construction is seen to advantage in *Tr* II.1180–1, where the initial impression that *Pandarus* provides the subject is reinforced by the two subordinate clauses which follow. The sudden shift in construction delightfully enacts the moment of surprise as Criseyde in playful mood steals upon Pandarus with the boast 'Ye were caught er that ye wiste' (1182).

For obvious reasons, pleonastic object-pronouns less often occur at the beginning of the second line; but there are some instances of contact repetition, especially in Chaucer's early lyrics, when the demonstrative pronoun *that* takes emphatic position before a verb:

> *ABC* 130. For certeynly my Faderes chastisinge, / That dar I nouht abiden in no wise
>
> *Pity* 99. My peyne is this, that what so I desire / That have I not
>
> *Pity* 103. What maner thing that may encrese my woo, / That have I redy
>
> *Lady* 44. And al that ever I wolde not, ywis, / That finde I redy to me evermore
>
> *Tr* IV.1294. what so ye me comaunde, / That wol I don
>
> *PardProl* 337. Our lige lordes seel on my patente, / That shewe I first

Pleonastic expression of the demonstrative is regularly accompanied by verbal inversion until the eighteenth century (see Visser, p. 520). It will be noticed that in *The Complaint unto Pity* and *A Complaint to his Lady* the construction occurs in the expression of the same romantic paradox.

Examples of distant repetition, in three or four lines of verse, are sometimes found in ME.:

> *GGK* 1851. For quat gome so is gorde with þis grene lace, / While he hit hade hemely halched aboute, / þer is no haþel vnder heuen tohewe hym þat myȝt
>
> *BD* 1326. And the book that I hadde red, / Of Alcione and Seys the kyng, / And of the goddes of slepyng, / I fond hyt in myn hond ful even
>
> *LGW* 1599. Medea, which that was so wis and fayr / That fayrer say there nevere man with ye, / He made hire don to Jason companye
>
> *MLT* 897. The sorwe that this Alla nyght and day / Maketh for his wyf, and for his child also, / Ther is no tonge that it telle may
>
> *WBProl* 737. Of Clitermystra, for hire lecherye, / That falsly made hire housbonde for to dye, / He redde it with ful good devocioun

The last example is included for the purpose of comparison. Here the seemingly pleonastic object-pronoun *it* is in fact equivalent to 'the tale' (compare *WBProl* 733–4), and the construction therefore exhibits the separation of the front-shifted genitive phrase 'Of Clitermystra' from its pronominal headword. In the other examples the repetition has a mainly structural function in providing reinforcement after a delay in the expression of subject and verb. Extraposition and repetition of the object in longer sentences would appear to be infrequent in Chaucer's poetry.

It remains to mention the pronominal repetition of an indirect object, which in ME. is often construed with an impersonal verb. In one form of pleonastic construction the front-shifted object is a noun phrase:

> *GGK* 1984. Vche mon þat he mette, he made hem a þonke
>
> *PP* B VI.70. And alkyn crafty men that konne lyuen in treuthe, / I shal fynden hem fode
>
> *Tr* I.331. Ye loveres! the konnyngeste of yow, / That serveth most ententiflich and best, / Hym tit as often harm therof as prow
>
> *SumT* 2014. An irous man, God sende hym litel myght
>
> *NPT* 3077. That oon of hem, in slepyng as he lay, / Hym mette a wonder dreem

In another form the indirect object is a prepositional phrase:

> *LGW* 2600. To Danao and Egistes also— / Althogh so be that they were brethren two, / For thilke tyme was spared no lynage— / It lykede hem to make a maryage

MillT 3563. But whan thou hast, for hire and thee and me, / Ygeten us thise knedyng tubbes thre

ClT 394. I seye that to this newe markysesse / God hath swich favour sent hire of his grace

PardT 621. Looke eek that to the kyng Demetrius, / The kyng of Parthes, as the book seith us, / Sente him a paire of dees of gold in scorn

MkT 2747. And to his doghter, that stood hym bisyde, / Which that he knew in heigh sentence habounde, / He bad hire telle hym what it signyfyde

Visser (pp. 520–1) in his notice of this construction includes some examples of pleonastic prepositional adjuncts in Elizabethan usage. This form of pleonasm is also found as early as Chaucer, in *MkT* 1999 'At Lucifer, though he as an angel were, / And nat a man, at hym wol I bigynne', where the iteration serves as a device of rhetorical heightening.

II ANACOLUTHON

Some examples of anacoluthon, and seeming anacoluthon, have already been given. In another form of *nominativus pendens* a generalising pronoun or a personal pronoun qualified by a relative clause is expressed first in the subjective and later in the sentence as a direct or indirect object-pronoun, as in Matt. xv.4 'He that curseth father or mother, let him die the death'. Constructions of this kind are found in OE. and thereafter in literary usage until at least the early seventeenth century (see Visser, pp. 60–1). Chaucer makes occasional use of them:

Havelok 76. Hwo-so dede hem wrong or lath, / Were it clerc, or were it kniht, / He dede hem sone to hauen riht

Tr I.857. For whoso list have helyng of his leche, / To hym byhoveth first unwre his wownde

Tr III.400. But he that goeth, for gold or for richesse, / On swich message, calle hym what the list

KnT 1553. That he that is my mortal enemy, / I serve hym as his squier povrely

MerchT 1320. He which that hath no wyf, I holde hym shent

MkT 2367. Allas, Fortune! she that whilom was / Dredeful to kynges and to emperoures, / Now gaureth al the peple on hire, allas!

The converse arrangement, with a shift from objective to subjective pronominal forms, occurs less often:

PF 623. Hym that she cheest, he shal hir han as swithe

Tr III.24. Algates hem that ye wol sette a-fyre, / They dreden shame, and vices they resygne

In both types of anacoluthon the form of the first pronoun is governed by its relation to the following verb and not the verb of the principal clause, which illustrates the tendency of English syntax, especially in earlier periods, 'to span only limited areas, and to make its laws of concord depend not so much on logic as on proximity' (Smith, p. 121). Such constructions may be used for emphasis and to suggest a particular meaning. *PF* 623, for example, can be seen as a expressive rearrangement of 'He shal han hir that cheest hym', by which Nature fairly balances female choice with male possession.

  OTHER FORMS OF PLEONASM

There are occasions in ME. writings when the genitive relation is expressed twice. The following relative clauses, for example, have a pleonastic genitive phrase at the end:

MerchT 1294. Of whiche he Theofraste is oon of tho

Caxton, *Charles* 38/19. of whome may not well be recounted the valyaunce of hym

As a device of emphasis, the repetition in *MerchT* 1294 is of a piece with the use of pronominal specification in the phrase 'he Theofraste' (see p. 62 above). More frequent in Chaucer's poetry are constructions in which a front-shifted genitive phrase is followed later by one or more pleonastic possessive adjectives:

Tr III.496. Or of what wight that stant in swich disjoynte, / His wordes alle, or every look, to poynte

Tr III.1548. Criseyde also, right in the same wyse, / Of Troilus gan in hire herte shette / His worthynesse, his lust, his dedes wise

Tr V.1752. Of Troilus, this ilke noble knyght, / As men may in thise olde bokes rede, / Was seen his knyghthod and his grete myght

MLT 582. Sathan, that evere us waiteth to bigile, / Saugh of Custance al hire perfeccioun

MkT 2575. What nedeth it of kyng Anthiochus / To telle his hye roial magestee?

The construction is more concrete and personal than the use of the definite article required by modern logic. Chaucer does not appear to use the converse of this order, when the genitive phrase is a postmodifier:

77

Launfal 976. Her maydenes come ayens her, ry3t, / To take her styrop whan sche ly3t— / Of þe lady, Dame Tryamour

Adverbs, prepositions, and subordinating conjunctions are sometimes repeated for emphasis or reinforcement. The iterative temporal adverb in the following sentence, for example, is used emphatically: *PF* 82 'And than, foryeven al hir wikked dede, / Than shul they come into this blysful place'. Locative adverbs are occasionally repeated in particular collocations:

HF 1645. And such a smoke gan out wende / Out of his foule trumpes ende

LGW 1780. And in he cometh into a prive halke

Malory 38/22. he may draw oute thys swerde oute of the sheethe

These examples show a weakening of the adverb in combination with a preposition, and the treatment of this combination as a simple preposition (see *OED* s.v. *out of*). The opposite phenomenon, when a pleonastic preposition has adverbial force, is sometimes to be found in relative clauses in late ME. (see Visser, p. 407):

GenProl 41. And eek in what array that they were inne

Malory 587/35. for He shulde helpe us into whos servyse we were entred in

This construction resembles the non-pleonastic use of *inne* in sentences like *KnT* 1618 'And sle me in this wode ther I am inne', where the discontinuous group *ther . . . inne* is equivalent to 'in which'. Mustanoja (p. 348) quotes *RvT* 4229 'And on this goode wyf he leith on soore' as a comparable instance of pleonasm; but it is more likely that *leith on* is a transitive phrasal verb meaning 'to make vigorous attack, assail' (*OED* s.v. *lay* v.[1] 55b), here used in a special sense. Palsgrave (p. 601) gives two forms of the idiom: 'Laye on, lay on upon the jade'. The preposition *upon* in the second form, and the first *on* in the example from Chaucer, represent the original dative case of the object of attack.

The particle *that* is sometimes repeated in certain functions to clarify the structure of sentences. As a consecutive conjunction, it is rarely used pleonastically in Chaucer's poetry:

Tr III.1622. be war of this meschief, / That, there as thow now brought art in thy blisse, / That thow thiself ne cause it nat to misse

That is more often pleonastic when its function is to reintroduce a noun clause:

Amis 146. Treweþes to-gider þai gun pli3t, / While þai mi3t liue & stond / þat boþe bi day & bi ni3t, / In wele & wo, in wrong & ri3t, / þat þai schuld frely fond / To hold to-gider at eueri nede

78

HF 97. pray I Jesus God / That (dreme he barefot, dreme he shod), / That every harm that any man / Hath had, syth the world began, / Befalle hym therof

LGW 2273. To vouche-sauf that, for a month or tweye, / That Philomene, his wyves syster, myghte / On Progne his wyf but ones han a syghte

KnT 3075. 'Suster,' quod he, 'this is my fulle assent, / With al th'avys heere of my parlement, / That gentil Palamon, youre owene knyght, / That serveth yow with wille herte, and myght, / And ever hath doon syn ye first hym knewe, / That ye shul of youre grace upon hym rewe, / And taken hym for housbonde and for lord'

ClT 691. He wolde have wend that of som subttiltee, / And of malice, or for crueel corage, / That she hadde suffred this with sad visage *Is this meant to be exhaustive or not?*

See also *Tr* III.492–3, 506–11, IV.31–3, *KnT* 1462–7, 2857–60, *PrT* 583–5. Foulet (p. 337) regards this form of repetition in OFr. as a result of carelessness, but the examples above, notably the measured speech of Theseus, suggest an emphasis on structure rather than a disregard for it. Troilus uses the construction twice in similar contexts in his somewhat laboured discussion of predestination:

> but nedly, as they sayn,
> Byhoveth it that thynges whiche that falle,
> That they in certayn ben purveyed alle.   (*Tr* IV.1006–8)

> By which resoun men may wel yse
> That thilke thynges that in erthe falle,
> That by necessite they comen alle.   (*Tr* IV.1048–50)

On some occasions *that* is so overworked that its pleonastic use as a conjunctive pronoun is hardly noticeable:

> Forthi with al myn herte I yow biseke,
> If that yow list don ought for my preyere,
> And for that love which that I love yow eke,
> That er that I departe fro yow here,
> *That* of so good a confort and a cheere
> I may yow sen, that ye may brynge at reste
> Myn herte, which that is o poynt to breste.   (*Tr* IV.1632–8)

> There was swich tydyng overal and swich loos,
> That in an yle that called was Colcos,
> Beyonde Troye, estward in the se,
> *That* therin was a ram, that men mighte se,
> That hadde a fles of gold, that shon so bryghte
> That nowher was swich anothir syghte.   (*LGW* 1424–9)

In the first passage, as A. C. Spearing points out, 'the utterly colourless word *that* is repeated eight times'; but he defends Chaucer against the

79

charge of incompetence by arguing that the repetition 'serves to express [Criseyde's] embarrassed anxiety to convince, and to expose her lack of material capable of producing rational conviction' (1972, p. 150). It will be noticed also that in three instances *that* merely reinforces another conjunction, whereas in the second passage the functional load on the particle is intolerably heavy. It is difficult to defend the usage in *LGW* 1424–9, whose syntax suggests an unintentional fussiness.

II ANTICIPATION

The proleptic use of personal and demonstrative pronouns to refer to a noun clause later in the sentence occurs in various forms throughout the history of English, but only a few constructions of special interest need be mentioned here. *It* or a demonstrative pronoun is commonly found as an anticipatory object in ME. with verbs of perception and expression:

> *Havelok* 2410. Hwan his folk þat sau and herde, / Hou Robert with here louerd ferde
>
> *Patience* 530. For-þy penaunce and payne to-preue hit in syʒt / þat pacience is a noble poynt
>
> *BD* 1128. Hyt ys no nede to reherse it more, / How ye sawe hir first, and where
>
> *HF* 729. Geffrey, thou wost ryght wel this, / That every kyndely thyng that is / Hath a kyndely stede
>
> *Anel* 162. Alas! what herte myght enduren hit, / For routhe or wo, her sorwe for to telle?
>
> *Tr* II.647. That to byholde it was a noble game, / How sobrelich he caste down his yën
>
> *MerchT* 1503. That dar presume, or elles thenken it, / That his conseil sholde passe his lordes wit

Here the noun clause is in tag order, and the construction as a whole suggests a certain concreteness of expression. While the anticipatory object-pronoun in such sentences is now considered redundant, in expressions like 'I think it my duty to speak' and 'I find it easy to believe him', where the object is construed with a predicate noun or adjective, *it* is normally expressed in both medieval and modern English:

> *Tr* II.164. For trewelich I holde it gret deynte, / A kynges sone in armes wel to do
>
> *LGW* F 326. and holdest it folye / To serve Love

Although examples of non-expression are to be found in late ME. prose, Chaucer appears to avoid its use in his poetry. Visser (p. 481) cites *MLT* 699 'Hir thoughte a despit that he sholde take / So strange a creature unto his make', but here the noun clause is the subject of an impersonal verb.

There is one particular idiom, however, whose present form is 'to find it in one's heart (to do something)', in which non-expression of *it* was the rule until the early nineteenth century (see Visser, pp. 472–3):

> *CA* V.5180. That he at eny time sholde / Evere after in his herte finde / To falsen and to be unkinde
>
> *Tr* V.1696. and I ne kan ne may, / For al this world, withinne myn herte fynde / To unloven yow a quarter of a day

In *Tr* II.164–5 quoted above, the anticipated infinitive clause has its own subject ('*A kynges sone* in armes wel to do'). This appears to be an extension of the common ME. use of such clauses in existential sentences:

> *Tr* III.630. Now were it tyme a lady to gon henne
>
> *Knt* 1523. It is ful fair a man to bere hym evene
>
> *KnT* 2288. But it is good a man been at his large
>
> *ShipT* 31. as famulier was he / As it is possible any freend to be
>
> Malory 52/34. hit ys the custom of my contrey a knyght allweyes to kepe hys wepyn with hym

In MnE. 'inorganic *for*' is expressed before the subject of the infinitive, a usage first recorded in the fourteenth century. The Queen of Love is in the vanguard of new usage when she chides her husband for his harsh treatment of poor Geoffrey:

> *LGW* F 400. For, syr, yt is no maistrye for a lord / To dampne a man without answere of word, / And, for a lord, that is ful foul to use

The origin of 'inorganic *for*' has been variously explained (see Mustanoja, pp. 383–4). The example from Chaucer suggests that a desire to emphasise the subject and restrict its application (that is, 'especially for a lord') may have played a part in the development of the construction.

CONCRETE NOUN CLAUSES

If in a form of the anticipatory construction described at the beginning of the last section, 'I knew it, that he was a good man', *it* is replaced by a noun or pronoun referring to the subject of the noun clause, the result is a characteristic Early English sentence: 'I knew him, that he was a good man'. The construction is still familiar as an archaism in Biblical usage. As Kellner notes, the form of expression in Gen. i.4 'And God saw the light, that it was good' is more vivid than its modern equivalent 'And God saw that the light was good', for in it 'the verb "see" has a concrete object, in which a certain attribute is perceived' (p. 58). Concrete noun clauses occur most often with verbs of seeing and hearing, and in such cases the expression of both the object of perception and the perception itself may be used to emphasise that the object is directly present to the senses, or to suggest the order in which physical and mental impressions are received.

Here are some examples of ME. usage. The concrete object may be governed by either a verb or a preposition:

> *WedGawen* 355. She told me her name, by the rode, / That it was Dame Ragnelle
>
> *LGW* 1066. And saw the man, that he was lyk a knyght
>
> *NPT* 2929. Which causeth folk to dreden in hir dremes / Of arwes, and of fyr with rede lemes, / Of rede beestes, that they wol hem byte

The construction is more frequent in Chaucer's poetry with noun clauses introduced by *how*:

> *Havelok* 1060. Ful sone it was ful loude kid / Of Hauelok, hu he warp þe ston
>
> *Amis* 773. He seiȝe hem boþe in þat tide / Hou þai seten yfere
>
> *GGK* 2433. I schal se hit ofte, / When I ride in renoun, remorde to myseluen / þe faut and þe fayntyse of þe flesche crabbed, / How tender hit is to entyse teches of fylþe
>
> *BD* 515. He was war of me, how y stood / Before hym
>
> *HF* 293. But let us speke of Eneas, / How he betrayed hir, allas
>
> *Tr* IV.176. Ector, which that wel the Grekis herde, / For Antenor how they wolde han Criseyde
>
> *LGW* F 62. To seen this flour, how it wol go to reste
>
> *NPT* 3201. Herkneth thise blisful briddes how they synge, / And se the fresshe floures how they sprynge
>
> Malory 72/7. and saw the lady how she was there

The unification of distinct impressions is clearly seen in some of these examples, notably in *LGW* F 62, which is an apt expression of the narrator's tender regard for the daisy. Other examples illustrate how the form of such clauses as dependent exclamations might be exploited for the purpose of emphasis, as in *HF* 293–4 and *NPT* 3201–2, the latter delightfully capturing Chauntecleer's innocence at a moment of danger.

CHAPTER V

Ellipsis

Fullness of expression and economy of expression are complementary phenomena, and the present chapter is therefore intended in some measure to balance the preceding treatment of pleonasm. The constructions for consideration have been identified by comparison with alternative patterns of syntax in Chaucer's poetry. It follows that sentences like *Tr* III.806 'Horaste! allas, and falsen Troilus?' will not be dealt with, for all their conciseness, because they are not generally to be compared with any fuller forms of expression. In the following sections we shall consider the ellipsis of personal pronouns and verbs; the omission of relative pronouns is given separate treatment in Chapter 6. The fullest outline of pronominal and verbal ellipsis in previous studies of Chaucer's language is by Fritz Karpf (pp. 129–44). Margaret Schlauch (pp. 1108–12) gives particular attention to the omission of conjunctions, though it must be said that many of her examples are not strictly elliptical.

It is important not to confuse ellipsis with brevity or conciseness in the study of style. An attempt has been made in a recent study of *The Miller's Tale* to find in its syntax a clue to the teller's character. The Miller's 'vigorously pedestrian vision' of an amoral world governed by chance and physical instinct is said to find expression in a preference for co-ordination in constructing his sentences, in a corresponding inability to handle subordination convincingly, and in a fondness for ellipsis:

An attendant indication of the Miller's inability to arrange his subject matter with any degree of logical precision is his inclination toward the ellipsis of relational words . . . While a common feature of Chaucer's reproduction of colloquial discourse, the frequency of such asyndetic constructions in the *Miller's Tale* goes well beyond the usual contingencies of verbal characterization to depict a mind debilitated by its own squalid confusion. Thus, in the opening description of Nicholas' talents, the Miller omits a requisite relative pronoun, reducing a potential hypotactic construction to paratactic simplicity: 'With hym ther was dwellynge a poure scoler, / Hadde lerned art . . . .' (3190–91). Later, as he describes the preparations against the flood, the Miller hurriedly abuts idea to idea and in the process deletes not only the relative 'by which', but also a necessary preposition of means: 'His owene hand he made laddres thre, / To clymben by the ronges and the stalkes' (3624–5). (Jambeck, p. 79)

It is a bit hard on the Miller to accuse him of 'squalid confusion' for such familiar and trifling omissions as that of a relative pronoun, and rather misleading to describe the second example as elliptical. The phrase 'his owene hand' is an attested ME. idiom and does not require a preposition; phrases of this type derive from OE. instrumental constructions, and in ME. 'are used primarily as emphatic equivalents of "himself, herself", i.e., to intensify the subject-noun or pronoun' (Mustanoja, pp. 106–7). Nor is 'laddres thre to clymben' an elliptical variant of 'by which to climb'; the noun + infinitive construction, in which 'the infinitive specifies the use that is made or can be made of the thing denoted by the noun it modifies' (Visser, p. 981), is found as a normal pattern of syntax throughout the history of English and commonly occurs in Chaucer's poetry. Subsequent examples are either of the inverted consecutive construction, as in 'Unto his brest it raughte, it was so lowe' (3696), from which nothing has been deleted, or of such concise but grammatically complete forms of expression as 'Spek, sweete bryd, I noot nat where thou art' (3805)—a line which, by the way, shows how even dialogue is pressed into service in an attempt to read the poem as a dramatic monologue. While these constructions may well be conducive to the brevity and emphasis characteristic of the fabliau style, they are not elliptical; and this must affect our estimate of the claim that the Miller is unable 'to arrange his subject matter with any degree of logical precision'.

Certain constructions in Chaucer's poetry are elliptical only in their appearance, and can be explained by reference to other features of ME. syntax. Other constructions are elliptical, but the element left unexpressed cannot always be precisely identified. There is, for example, disagreement whether a personal or a relative pronoun is omitted in some sentences, though the principle of comparison with alternative forms of expression usually solves this problem for the purpose of stylistic inquiry. Constructions of the following kind present a similar difficulty in analysis:

> Anoon this god of slep abrayd
> Out of hys slep, and gan to goon,
> And dyde as he had bede hym doon;
> ʌ Took up the dreynte body sone
> And bar hyt forth to Alcione.   (*BD* 192–6)

In headless clauses such as this, is the ellipsis of a subject-pronoun or of the co-ordinating conjunction *and*? Although the former is the more likely possibility, the treatment of headless clauses will be deferred until

Chapter 7, where they can be considered in relation to other forms of asyndetic construction.

 SUBJECT-PRONOUNS

In an examination of the ellipsis of subjects and objects it may be assumed for the purpose of description that, were the exponents of these grammatical categories to be expressed, they would be personal pronouns. Ellipsis of the subject in ME. has been surveyed by W. F. S. Roberts, whose scheme of classification is adopted by Mustanoja (pp. 138–44); Visser (pp. 4ff.) provides a full historical outline.

Co-ordinate Clauses

The form of ellipsis in a sentence like 'I saw my friend and (I) called to him' is so common in all periods and styles of English as to be unremarkable. In ME. there are also several types of elliptical co-ordination which differ from modern usage and may be represented by the sentence 'I saw my friend and (he) called to me'. Karpf (pp. 135–44) and the authors of the ME. studies mentioned above describe these constructions with reference to the syntactical function of the word or phrase in the preceding clause that is thought to supply the subject of the elliptical clause. This scheme leads to a certain complexity, and it will be simpler in the first instance to classify the varieties of elliptical co-ordination in Chaucer's poetry according to the person and number of the unexpressed subject, beginning with constructions in the singular.

The omission of the first person singular subject-pronoun is not frequently met with:

Havelok 14. Fil me a cuppe of ful god ale; / And ∧ wile drinken, er y spelle

PP B. V.172. thei taken hem togyderes, / And do me faste Frydayes to bred and to water, / And ∧ am chalanged in the chapitelhous as I a childe were

Tr III.1619. it is me lief; / And ∧ am as glad as man may of it be

More common in dialogue is the ellipsis of the second person singular:

Amis 1444. if it bitide so / þat þe bitide care oþer wo, / & of min help ∧ hast nede

HF 652. For when thy labour don al ys, / And ∧ hast mad alle thy rekenynges

HF 2012. Such routhe hath he of thy distresse, / That thou suffrest debonairly— / And ∧ wost thyselven outtirly / Disesperat of alle blys

Tr I.916. And som, thow seydest, hadde a blaunche fevere, / And ∧ preydest God he sholde nevere kevere

But it is in the third person singular that subject-pronouns are most often omitted in co-ordinate clauses in ME. Mustanoja observes that 'the connection between the subject and the verb is somehow less close in the third person than in the first or second' (p. 139), which may owe something to psychology and also to the simple fact that only two of the terms in a three-term system need to be used with some consistency in order to maintain the system. Here are some representative examples of this form of ellipsis:

> *Havelok* 1371. For i ne misdede him neuere nouht, / And ∧ haueth me to sorwe brouht
>
> *Gamelyn* 197. And ther he herd a frankeleyn wayloway synge, / And ∧ bigan bitterly his hondes for to wrynge
>
> *CA* III.1331. I rede a tale, and ∧ telleth this
>
> *Tr* II.333. I se hym deyen, ther he goth upryght, / And ∧ hasteth hym with al his fulle myght
>
> *Tr* IV.341. And shortly, so his peynes hym torente, / And ∧ wex so mat
>
> *LGW* F 90. That, as an harpe obeieth to the hond / And ∧ maketh it soune after his fyngerynge
>
> *LGW* 2308. The ores pullen forth the vessel faste, / And into Trace ∧ aryveth at the laste
>
> *WBProl* 540. That made his face often reed and hoot / For verray shame, and ∧ blamed hymself
>
> *PardT* 885. it happed hym, par cas, / To take the botel ther the poyson was, / And ∧ drank
>
> *NPT* 3378. And syen the fox toward the grove gon, / And ∧ bar upon his bak the cok away

The elliptical construction is sometimes equivalent to a non-restrictive relative clause, as in *LGW* F 90. Of particular interest are those examples in which the subject is to be understood from a preceding accusative and infinitive construction. If co-ordination were to be retained in similar sentences today, the verb of the elliptical clause would also have to be in the infinitive. The shift to the indicative mood in ME. usage is not so logical, but it may give a more graphic touch to the narrative, as in *Tr* II.333-4 and *NPT* 3378-9.

Third person singular subject-pronouns tend to be omitted in certain contexts. Some ME. writers are partial to ellipsis after clauses having a formal subject:

> *HSynne* 171. Hyt was onys a munke, and ∧ had a celle
>
> *HSynne* 501. þere was a wycche, and ∧ made a bagge
>
> *Tr* II.1111. Ther is right now come into town a gest, / A Greek espie, and ∧ telleth newe thinges
>
> *GenProl* 477. A good man was ther of religioun, / And ∧ was a povre persoun of a toun

Here again the elliptical construction has the force of a relative clause. This usage is frequently met with in *Handlyng Synne*, for example, but only occasionally in Chaucer's poetry. More widespread is the use of ellipsis before the verb *said*:

Havelok 838. On Hauelok was al hise þouht, / And ʌ seyde

Emaré 763. Then was the stewardes herte wo, / And ʌ sayde

CA II.2738. And with that word his hewe fadeth, / And ʌ seide

Tr II.326. With that the teris bruste out of his yën, / And ʌ seide

LGW 2314. For which hire herte agros, and ʌ seyde thus

KnT 2432. And with that soun he herde a murmurynge / Ful lowe and dym, and ʌ seyde thus

Here the subject is to be understood from a possessive noun or adjective, less often an object, in the preceding clause. Another context in which ellipsis occurs is after direct speech:

Emaré 452. 'Modyr, y wylle have thys may!' / And forth ʌ gan her lede

Tr III.69. 'Ye, swete herte? allas, I may nought rise, / To knele and do yow honour in som wyse.' / And ʌ dressed hym upward

Tr III. 1517. 'As fayn wolde I as ye that it were so, / As wisly God myn herte brynge at reste!' / And hym in armes ʌ tok, and ofte keste

ClT 1056. 'Now knowe I, dere wyf, thy stedfastnesse,'— / And hire in armes ʌ took and gan hire kesse

FranklT 1619. 'It is ynogh, and farewel, have good day!' / And ʌ took his hors

Mustanoja says that in such instances the subject is to be understood 'from a previous first singular subject and also from a more distant third singular subject of the verb introducing the words spoken' (p. 142), and notes that the construction is most often recorded in Chaucer.

Plural subject-pronouns are omitted less frequently than singular forms in ME. The first person plural is omitted in *GenProl* 785 'Us thoughte it was noght worth to make it wys, / And ʌ graunted hym withouten moore avys', and the second person plural in *Tr* V.939 'syn that I am youre man,— / And ʌ ben the first of whom I seche grace'. Both of these forms of ellipsis are rare. Once again, the subject is more often left unexpressed in third person constructions:

Arthour L 632. A riche man was in Engelonde / And hadde a good womman to wyue / And ʌ lyued togedre in clene lyue

Emaré 199. Her norysse, that hyghte Abro, / Wyth her she goth forth also, / And ʌ wer sette in a chare

BD 360. Ther overtok y a gret route / Of huntes and eke of foresteres,

/ With many relayes and lymeres, / And ∧ hyed hem to the forest faste

Tr I.86. and generaly was spoken, / That Calkas traitour fled was and allied / With hem of Grece, and ∧ casten to be wroken / On hym

Tr III.453. And by hire bothe avys, as was the beste, / ∧ Apoynteden ful warly in this nede

MLT 621. ther was gret moornyng / Among the people, and ∧ seyn they kan nat gesse

The subject is usually to be understood from a previous plural or collective noun or a compound subject. Karpf (p. 139) gives *Tr* I.88 as an instance of the subject being supplied by a pronoun in a prepositional phrase ('With hem of Grece'); but it is the Trojans, not the Greeks, who desire revenge.

b *Significant Imprecision*

Some stylistic implications of the forms of ellipsis described above may now be considered. C. T. Onions writes:

> Ellipsis plays a great part in English, as in many languages. It is common to all styles of speaking and writing. In poetical and rhetorical language it often lends dignity and impressiveness, with something of an archaic flavour; to colloquial speech it gives precision and brevity, and saves time and trouble. (p. 4)

So far as the ellipsis of subject-pronouns in Chaucer's poetry is concerned, the brevity so achieved is not restricted to colloquial expression, and may be used to suggest rapid action by bringing in the verb as soon as possible. For instance, in *LGW* 1243 'How Eneas hath with the queen ygon / Into the cave; and ∧ demede as hem liste' the ellipsis of the plural subject testifies to a sense of urgency on the part of the lovers. Of greater interest are two passages from the same poem in which a third person singular subject is omitted. The first passage refers to Jason and Medea, and the second to Theseus and Ariadne:

> And hereupon at nyght they mette in-feere,
> And ∧ doth his oth, and goth with hire to bedde.　(1643–4)

> There feste they, there daunce they and synge;
> And in his armes ∧ hath this Adryane.　(2157–8)

It may not be altogether a coincidence that this form of ellipsis should occur in similar contexts, where it suggests the suddenness and inevitability of romantic conquest. The shift from plural to unexpressed masculine singular is arresting in its abrupt denial of equality to the participants; it is as if our attention were so taken for granted to rest on the hero that formal reference to him was felt to be superfluous. Perhaps

88

on a small scale this usage reflects Chaucer's greater interest in bad men than in good women in several of the legends.

It has been suggested that ellipsis gives 'precision and brevity', but the omission of subject-pronouns in Chaucer's poetry is often more tellingly used to effect what A. C. Spearing describes as 'significant imprecision':

> One common element in conversational language is a kind of significant imprecision, intolerable in prose. It may involve ambiguity of reference, or perhaps running together two different constructions, so that one statement changes almost imperceptibly into another in mid-sentence; and there are many other kinds of imprecision, which form important parts of the way conversation conveys meaning and emotion. Chaucer is highly sensitive to these significant imprecisions, and often uses them in *Troilus and Criseyde*. (1976, p. 14)

As an example of ambiguity we might consider *Tr* V848 'Criseyde, at shorte wordes for to telle, / Welcomed hym, and down hym by hire sette'. What is the subject of the verb *sette*? Karpf (p. 135) says that it is to be understood from the preceding reflexive object-pronoun *hym*; according to this analysis, Diomede seats himself beside Criseyde. It is perhaps more likely, however, in view of *Tr* II.91 'And with that word she doun on bench hym sette', that *hym* is not reflexive and that the subject of the sentence does not change: 'Criseyde welcomed him and seated him beside her'. If so, the line adds an interesting detail to the picture of Criseyde in the Greek camp.

Ellipsis of the subject achieves a significant imprecision in the following passage from *The Book of the Duchess*, in which Morpheus conveys the drowned king Ceyx to his wife:

> Anoon this god of slep abrayd
> Out of hys slep, and gan to goon,
> And dyde as he had bede hym doon;
> Took up the dreynte body sone
> And bar hyt forth to Alcione
> Hys wif the quene, ther as she lay
> Ryght even a quarter before day,
> And ʌ stood ryght at hyr beddes fet.   (192–9)

Here 'one statement changes almost imperceptibly into another in mid-sentence'. Although the phrase 'this god of slep' seems at first to provide the subject of each co-ordinate clause in this sequence, it is clear on reflection that the subject of *stood* in the last line must be understood from *hyt*, 'the dreynte body' animated by Morpheus. The silent change of subject serves as a device of ambiguity enabling Chaucer to avoid specification of the actor, and may be said to enact the process of transformation.

Chaucer employs an unusual form of ellipsis to describe the meeting of Palamon and Arcite in battle in *The Knight's Tale*:

Tho chaungen gan the colour in hir face,
Right as the hunters in the regne of Trace,
That stondeth at the gappe with a spere,
Whan hunted is the leon or the bere,
And hereth hym come russhyng in the greves,
And ʌ breketh bothe bowes and the leves,
And ʌ thynketh, 'Heere cometh my mortal enemy!'

                                          (1637–43)

As J. A. W. Bennett explains, '*breketh* is syntactically parallel with *hereth* . . . *thinketh*, but would be more naturally used of the beast' (p. 126). That is, the construction exhibits a form of double ellipsis, with the established subject being abandoned in line 1642 after the expression of *hym*, which is normal enough, and then silently resumed in the next line. The double ellipsis serves to strengthen the emphasis on action in the series of co-ordinate clauses with which this epic simile builds to a climax. At the same time, the lack of pronominal specification, with the point of view shifting unexpectedly from the hunter to the hunted and back again, momentarily blurs the distinction between the opponents. 'Unusually in Chaucer,' writes A. C. Spearing, 'at this moment of excitement, the syntax takes on a Shakespearean ambiguity' (1966, p. 170).

The double ellipsis in this passage is uncommon, but perhaps not unique, in Chaucer's poetry. A comparable instance is possibly to be found in the description of an alchemical fraud in *The Canon's Yeoman's Tale*:

And in his sleve (as ye biforen-hand
Herde me telle) he hadde a silver teyne.
He slyly took it out, this cursed heyne,
Unwityng this preest of his false craft,
And in the pannes botme he hath it laft;
And in the water ʌ rombled to and fro,
And wonder pryvely ʌ took up also
The coper teyne, noght knowynge this preest,
And hidde it, and hym hente by the breest,
And to hym spak, and thus seyde in his game.   (1317–26)

The verb *rombled* in line 1322 is normally taken to mean 'made a rumbling noise (by groping)' (*Glossary* s.v. *rumbelen*); but this sense is rare (see *OED* s.v. *rumble* v.[1] 4a, which cites this line as the earliest instance), especially when the verb collocates with phrases like 'to and fro', 'up and down'. It is more likely that the rumbling is caused by the piece of silver than by the canon, and that the construction of lines 1321–3 is therefore as follows, with the unexpressed subject-pronouns in brackets:

Line	Subject	Object
1321	he	it
1322	(it)	
1323	(he)	

90

Simply not the case

This is the same pattern found in *The Knight's Tale*, except that here the object-pronoun does not belong to an accusative and infinitive construction. These omissions, occurring at the crucial point of substitution, may be seen to follow a form of action in their syntactical reflection of the canon's sleight-of-hand. One co-ordinate clause follows another in breathless succession to keep pace with his movements, and at the very moment of deception, as the unwitting priest looks on, the syntax loses its sharp focus into two abruptly elliptical clauses.

In conclusion, it may be noted that double ellipsis of this kind sometimes occurs elsewhere in ME. poetry, though not necessarily with an effect of significant imprecision:

> þe burne blessed hym bilyue, and þe bredez passed—
> Prayses þe porter bifore þe prynce kneled,
> ʌ Gef hym God and goud day, þat Gawayn he saue—
> And ʌ went on his way with his wyʒe one. (*GGK* 2071-4)

That is, 'Gawain praised the porter, (the porter) wished him well, and (Gawain) went on his way'. The result is a degree of conciseness that is fairly typical of alliterative verse. Notice also the ellipsis of a relative pronoun in line 2072 and the form of the salutation in the next line, which has been described as 'an elliptical and distorted, perhaps idiomatic, way of saying "gave him (as farewell) *good day* and *God save you*"' (Davis, p. 125).

Other Constructions

With the exception of some special constructions to be considered here, ellipsis of the subject normally occurs in co-ordinate clauses in Chaucer's poetry. He appears not to have favoured this form of omission in complex sentences, though instances are occasionally to be found in the writings of his contemporaries when the subjects of the clauses are co-referential:

Launfal 622. Syr Launfal schuld be stward of halle / Forto agye hys gestes alle, / For ʌ cowþe of largesse

PP B XII.55. And, for thei suffren & se so many nedy folkes, / And loue hem nouʒt as owre lorde byt ʌ lesen her soules

Mustanoja (p. 141) cites *GenProl* 218 'For he hadde power of confessioun, / As seyde hymself, moore than a curat', but this is a special form of construction in which a personal pronoun reinforced by *self* functions as the subject. The usage is fairly common in Chaucer's poetry:

Tr III.369. Sith I so loth was that thiself it wiste

Tr IV.600. Thenk ek Fortune, as wel thiselven woost, / Helpeth hardy man to his enprise

PardProl 429. But though myself be gilty in that synne

PardProl 459. For though myself be a ful vicous man

CYT 984. But it a feend be, as hymselven is

91

The construction is also found in principal clauses:

Havelok 2042. Mi-self shal dubben him to kniht
BD 34. Myselven can not telle why
Tr II.1201. Myself to medes wol the lettre sowe
Tr IV.21. Iwis, hemself sholde han the vilanye
WBProl 175. This is to seyn, myself have been the whippe
Thop 915. Hymself drank water of the well

Here for comparison are clauses in which a personal subject-pronoun is expressed:

Orfeo A 29. Him-self he lerned for-to harp
BD 676. Myself I wolde have do the same
GenProl 803. I wol myselven goodly with yow ryde
KnT 1835. Ye woot yourself she may nat wedden two
MLT 434. For she hirself wolde al the contree lede
MerchT 1460. I woot myselven best what I may do

If any difference is to be seen in the use of these alternative constructions, it is possibly that non-expression tends to belong to a more familiar style.

One other form of variation between expression and non-expression of the subject may be mentioned. The use of *it* to anticipate a noun clause in sentences containing a subject complement, as in 'It is right that we should go', is common in all periods. In ME. there is also a variant form with suppression of the anticipatory subject-pronoun, as in *HF* 1614 'Therfore is ryght that we ben quyt' (see Visser, pp. 19–20). Non-expression is more frequent when the predicate noun or adjective is front-shifted:

Havelok 843. Betere is þat þu henne gonge
BD 1266. And pitee were I shulde sterve
LGW 1311. She kneleth, cryeth, that routhe is to devyse
MkT 2489. Greet wonder is how that he koude or myghte / Be domesman of hire dede beautee

This usage is common with noun clauses introduced by *though* in assertions and rhetorical questions:

Havelok 124. No selcouth is, þouh me be wo
Isumbras 76. What wondur was thowgh hym were wo?
Tr II.749. What wondir is though he of me have joye?
Tr V.62. What wondir is, though that hire sore smerte?
WBT 1102. That litel wonder is thogh I walwe and wynde

For expression of the anticipatory subject compare:

Mars 182. What wonder ys it then, thogh I besette / My servise on
    such on?
Anel 148. gret wonder was hit noon / Thogh he were fals
MLT 267. Allas! what wonder is it thogh she wepte?

II   OBJECT-PRONOUNS

Omission of the object is less frequent in all periods of English than
omission of the subject. In attempting to identify this form of ellipsis, we
must take into account both the absolute use of transitive verbs (see
Visser, pp. 141–52) and obsolete patterns of word-order. ME. usage sanc-
tioned considerable freedom in the placing of verbs with a common
object. The object might come between two verbs in broken order, as in
Tr III.1767 'To cerclen hertes alle, and faste bynde', or before both of
them, as in *Anel* 6 'Be present, and my song contynue and guye'. These
forms of construction are not elliptical, and will not be considered here.
Ellipsis of the object may be said to occur if one of the verbs takes an
adjunct that is not applicable to the other, as in 'He scolded the boy and
sent (him) to bed':

Havelok 1418. þat he me sholde bere / Vnto þe se, and drenchen ʌ
    inne
Guy II 5707. He toke a mantell of ryche colowre / And caste ʌ on Gye
    for hys honowre
Tr III.1737. And by the hond ful ofte he wolde take / This Pandarus,
    and into gardyn lede ʌ

Ellipsis also occurs when an indirect object is to be understood from a
previously expressed direct object, and *vice versa*:

Arthour A 5185. Agreuein dede also / Mani slouȝ and dede ʌ wo
Havelok 83. And hwo-so dide maydne shame / Of hire bodi, or
    brouht ʌ in blame
KnT 1248. That may me helpe or doon ʌ confort in this
MkT 2161. To which ymage bothe yong and oold / Comanded he to
    loute, and have ʌ in drede

Ohlander (1943, pp. 119–22) gives further examples, and he also notes (pp.
124–5) the omission of an object-pronoun that is to be understood from an
adjacent possessive adjective:

Peace 19. Bot now ther is no mannes herte spared / To love and serve
    ʌ and wirche thi plesaunce

BD 769. Al this I putte in his servage, / As to my lord, and dide ∧ homage

On the other hand, these sentences may illustrate the absolute use of verbs normally taking a direct and indirect object respectively.

Mention may also be made of economical constructions such as 'He saw, and asked the price of, the book', which is not elliptical and does not depart from the normal order of words. Ohlander (1943, p. 124) quotes a line from Laʒamon's *Brut*, 'To visite and speke with þe King of Engelond', as an example of ellipsis, but the structure is the same as that in modern usage. Compare *MkT* 2098 'He slow, and rafte the skyn of the leoun'. A similar sentence-pattern appears in 'He saw, and was seen by, his friends', where a transitive verb is used first in the active voice and then in the passive:

WBProl 551. I hadde the bettre leyser for to pleye, / And for to se, and eek for to be seye / Of lusty folk

Although the metrical separation of *seye* and *of* suggests a less logical analysis than that made at the present day, the structure is the same in both periods.

VERBS

As Karpf (pp. 129–35) has shown, the ellipsis of verbs is quite common in Chaucer's poetry. In this section we shall consider the ellipsis of the copula *be*, of verbs of motion, and of non-finite verbs; but the ME. equivalents of sentences like 'John a manager?', 'The more the merrier', and 'What if he wins?', which have no comparable fuller forms, will not be dealt with. Since the nature of verbal ellipsis is usually fairly obvious, the omissions are not marked in the following outline.

Verbless Clauses

When a form of the copula *be* is omitted, the construction is known in modern grammar as a verbless clause (see Quirk and Greenbaum, pp. 312–13). Verbless clauses of the following kind are common in ME. poetry:

Havelok 606. 'Goddot!' quath Grim, 'þis ure eir'

HF 502. But this as sooth as deyth, certeyn, / Hyt was of gold

KnT 2761. This al and som, that Arcita moot dye

ClT 56. But this his tale, which that ye may heere

NPT 3057. Mordre wol out, this my conclusioun

This form of ellipsis, which may represent the assimilation of *is* to the demonstrative pronoun *this*, most often occurs in clauses of preparation or summary in Chaucer's poetry. For expression of the copula compare *LGW* 998 'For this is al and som, it was Venus'. Ellipsis is occasionally found in similar passive constructions, such as *Tr* III.936 'This seyd by hem that ben nought worth two fecches'.

Chaucer and other ME. poets frequently omit the copula in co-ordinate clauses. Sentences of the type 'She is the queen, and I (am) her subject' occur mainly in dialogue:

Havelok 2803. þat Aþelwold / Was king of [al] þis kunerike, / And ye his eyr

BD 1037. For certes she was, that swete wif, / My suffisaunce, my lust, my lyf, / Myn hap, myn hele, and al my blesse, / My worldes welfare, and my goddesse, / And I hooly hires and everydel

Tr III.272. May thynken that she is my nece deere, / And I hire em, and traitour eke yfeere

Tr V.169. Ther ben so worthi knyghtes in this place, / And ye so fayr, that everich of hem alle / Wol peynen hym to stonden in youre grace

LGW F 321. Yt is my relyke, digne and delytable, / And thow my foo, and al my folk werreyest

MerchT 2315. 'I am a kyng, it sit me noght to lye.' / 'And I,' quod she, 'a queene of Fayerye'

Notice the pattern of double ellipsis in *LGW* F 321–2, with subject and verb expressed in the first clause, subject only in the second, and verb only in the third, which achieves a conciseness that is no longer obtainable. The verbless clause in these examples is co-ordinate with a clause of similar structure in which the copula is expressed. There are also instances in which the first clause has a different structure or contains a different verb:

Gowther 37. When he had weddyd that medyn schene, / And sche duches, withowt wene, / A mangeré con thei make

Tr III.278. And seyn that I the werste trecherie / Dide in this cas, that evere was bigonne, / And she forlost, and thow right nought ywonne

Tr III.915. Ye knowe ek how it is youre owen knyght, / And that bi right ye moste upon hym triste, / And I al prest to fecche hym whan yow liste

LGW 838. Allas! to bidde a woman gon by nyghte / In place there as peril falle myghte! / And I so slow! allas, I ne hadde be / Here in this place a furlong wey or ye

The verbless clause in sentences of this kind tends to assume a more independent character, and resembles a form of expression in MnE. noted by C. T. Onions:

The equivalent of an absolute clause exemplified in the following quotation is rare and poetical:

How can ye chant ye little birds,
    And I sae fu' o' care?—BURNS

But in illiterate language there is a similar construction with the
accusative: 'How could the room be cleaned, *and me with my
rheumatism?* (p. 76)

The origin of this construction is obscure; it may have arisen naturally
from the extension of co-ordinate verbless clauses to exclamatory and
interrogative sentences. For expression of the copula in what appears to
be a related construction used in a fifteenth-century mystery play, compare *Shearmen* 224 'Brothur, where hast thow byn soo long, / And hit ys
soo cold this nyght?'

To be considered next are verbless descriptive clauses that depend on
previous expression of the copula, in sentences like 'Her hair was black,
her eyes (were) green'. The construction is so familiar that only a few
examples need be given:

> *Isumbras* 250. His lady is wyte as wales bone, / Here lere bryghte to
>   se upon
> *GenProl* 151. Ful semyly hir wympul pynched was, / Hir nose
>   tretys, hir eyen greye as glas, / Hir mouth ful smal, and therto
>   softe and reed
> *GenProl* 200. He was a lord ful fat and in good poynt; / His eyen
>   stepe, and rollynge in his heed, / That stemed as a forneys of a
>   leed; / His boutes souple, his hors in greet estaat
> *KnT* 2167. His nose was heigh, his eyen bright citryn, / His lippes
>   rounde, his colour was sangwyn
> *MLT* 167. Hir herte is verray chambre of hoolynesse, / Hir hand
>   ministre of fredam for almesse

Notice the chiastic pattern of expression and non-expression in *KnT*
2167–8. Chaucer's usage does not greatly differ from that of the present
day; but the construction in the following examples is no longer found:

> *GenProl* 456. Hir hosen weren of fyn scarlet reed, / Ful streite
>   yteyd, and shoes ful moyste and newe
> *GenProl* 491. Wyd was his parisshe, and houses fer asonder

In such sentences a possessive adjective is now felt to be necessary
before the subject of the verbless clause. This could replace the co-
ordinating conjunction in the first example, bringing it into line with
the more usual asyndetic form illustrated above, but not in the second; if
the parish belongs to the parson, the houses belong to the parish, which
Chaucer could not express without risk of ambiguity, since the possessive adjective *his* serves in ME. as both masculine and neuter ('its').

In these examples the copula has previously been expressed, so that
the ellipsis is essentially a matter of non-repetition. Verbless clauses
sometimes follow other forms of construction:

KnT 1362. That lene he wex and drye as is a shaft; / His eyen
    holwe, and grisly to beholde, / His hewe falow and pale as
    asshen colde

KnT 2133. And lik a grifphon looked he aboute, / With kempe
    heeris on his browes stoute; / Hys lymes grete, his brawnes
    harde and stronge, / His shuldres brode, his armes rounde and
    longe

In the first example it might be felt that the verb *wex* is simply not
repeated, but the second clearly illustrates the nature of the construction. The expressions in *KnT* 2135–6 can only be verbless clauses, and
not elliptical forms of the preceding prepositional phrase or forms of
inversion parallel to 'his browes stoute'.

    It remains to mention one or two uses of verbless clauses which differ
from modern practice. For example, the copula is sometimes omitted in
formations with a past participle:

Tr I.129. And whil she was dwellynge in that cite, / Kepte hir estat,
    and both of yonge and olde / Ful wel biloved, and wel men of
    hir tolde

GenProl 48. And therto hadde he riden, no man ferre, / As wel in
    cristendom as in hethenesse, / And evere honoured for his
    worthynesse

The following construction is similarly inconsequential by present-day
standards:

HF 1830. We ben shrewes, every wyght, / And han delyt in wikked-
    nesse, / As goode folk han in godnesse; / And joye to be
    knowen shrewes, / And ful of vice and wikked thewes

There is an ellipsis here, but of what? Are these exuberant petitioners to
Fame saying that they *are* full of vice, or that they *enjoy* being so, or that
they enjoy being *known* to be so? Perhaps all at once, the imprecision
aptly reflecting a mischievous delight in wicked behaviour and poor
reputation. Expression of the verbal form *ben* would not distinguish the
first two possibilities and would exclude the third.

Verbs of Motion

Chaucer often omits finite and infinitive verbs of motion (see Karpf, pp.
130–2). Ellipsis of the infinitive in sentences like 'I will (go) to sea', in
which an auxiliary verb is used with an adjunct indicating the direction
of travel, is common from the OE. period until early modern times.
Although, as Visser (p. 163) points out, this usage is of long standing in
the Germanic languages and properly constitutes a complete construction, it is convenient to regard it as elliptical by comparison with fuller
forms. The auxiliary verbs most frequently used are *may, must, shall,*
and *will*:

Amis 996. No ferþer he no miȝt

Gowther 233. For Y wyll to Rome or that Y rest

Launfal 78. He most to his beryynge

HF 187. And seyde he moste unto Itayle

RvT 4117. For it was nyght, and further myghte they noght

FrT 1636. Thou shalt with me to helle yet to-nyght

ShipT 361. Oure abbot wole out of this toun anon

Mustanoja suggests that the construction is 'characteristic of lively, impulsive narration' (p. 544). There is also a tendency for this use of auxiliary verbs to reinforce notions of resolution and obligation. In *The Man of Law's Tale*, for example, Constance reluctantly takes leave of her parents with the words 'I shal to Surrye' (279), and then 'Allas! unto the Barbre nacioun / I moste anoon' (281–2). Shortly after this the narrator concludes his description of the tearful parting with the fatalistic comment 'But forth she moot, wher-so she wepe or synge' (294). The use of auxiliary verbs in this scene underscores the sense of obligation and necessity that informs the tale as a homiletic romance.

The emphasis is more firmly on lively and impulsive action when finite verbs of motion are omitted, usually before a locative adverb:

Havelok 1675. þe stede, þat he onne sat, / Smot Ubbe [þo] with spures faste, / And forth awey

Gowther 325. Syr Gwother up and in con gwon

BD 356. I was ryght glad, and up anoon, / Took my hors, and forth I wente

Tr I.126. And took hire leve, and hom, and held hire stille

Tr II.787. That, right anon as cessed is hire lest, / So cesseth love, and forth to love a newe

Tr II.1492. Whan this was don, this Pandare up anon

Tr III.547. Now is ther litel more for to doone, / But Pandare up

Tr III.1094. But al was hust, and Pandare up as faste

It is appropriate that ellipsis with the adverb *up*, which later developed into a verb in its own right (see *OED* s.v. v. 5b), should often occur in passages describing the activities of Pandarus, where it helps to convey an impression of vigour and abruptness. This is a common form of emphatic expression in ME. The usual punctuation of *BD* 356–7 in modern editions gives instead the phrasal verb *took up*, but the consequent implication of lifting (see *OED* s.v. *take* v. 90, and compare *BD* 195) does not make good sense with reference to a horse. It is more in keeping with the urgency of this passage to have the ellipsis of a verb of motion, followed by an asyndetic co-ordinate clause.

98

Under this heading we shall consider the ellipsis of infinitives and past participles. The omission of an infinitive after a co-ordinate auxiliary verb like *shall* or *will*, as in 'I love you, and always shall', is quite common in Chaucer's poetry (see Karpf, pp. 133–4). It is a notable feature of his love poetry, in affirmations of loyalty, belief, and intention:

> *HSynne* 10067. þys y beleue, and euer y shal
>
> *Lady* 30. Hir love I best, and shal, whyl I may dure
>
> *Tr* III.713. As wys as I the serve, / And evere bet and bet shal, til I sterve
>
> *Tr* V.615. And here I dwelle out caste from alle joie, / And shal, til I may sen hire eft in Troie
>
> *LGW* F 56. And I love it, and ever ylike newe, / And evere shal, til that myn herte dye
>
> *MerchT* 2323. Yow love I best, and shal, and oother noon

Expressions of this kind are frequently met with from OE. to early MnE. (see Visser, pp. 1840–1); in them the prominence given to the auxiliary verbs calls attention to how the speaker regards the action which he chooses, or feels compelled, to perform. The construction is also found with a preterite verb in the preceding clause:

> *Tr* III.1514. Thus seyde I nevere er this, ne shal to mo
>
> *Tr* V.157. I loved never womman here-biforn, / As paramours, ne nevere shal no mo
>
> *ClT* 823. I nevere heeld me lady ne mistresse, / But humble servant to youre worthynesse, / And ever shal, whil that my lyf may dure

It may be noted, with regard to the first two examples, that the iteration of the subject-pronoun in negative constructions ('nor shall I') is a fairly recent development.

The infinitive of the copula is omitted in expressions of the type 'I am yours, and ever shall (be)' (see Visser, pp. 1843–4). This construction, which lasted until the seventeenth century, is generally used to express endurance and continuity:

> *HSynne* 8225. Oure myȝt ys noght, no neuer shal
>
> *CMundi* T 14661. For we ben oon & shul euermore
>
> *CA* VIII.2277. Began mi love, of which myn hevynesse / Is now and evere schal, bot if I spede
>
> *HF* 81. And he that mover ys of al / That is and was and ever shal
>
> *Tr* III.1607. Whos I am al, and shal, tyl that I deye
>
> *Tr* V.832. Oon of the beste entecched creature / That is, or shal, whil that the world may dure

Chaucer avoids the kind of illogicality to be seen in the first example (= 'nor ever shall be *nothing*'). Sometimes the ellipsis follows expression of the copula in the preterite. In *Troilus and Criseyde* this usage occurs with the separation of the lovers, who at the end of Book IV speak of their love in terms not of present and future, but of past and future:

> *Tr* IV.1655. I nevere unto Criseyde, / Syn thilke day I saugh hire first with yë, / Was fals, ne nevere shal til that I dye
>
> *Tr* IV.1680. That I was youre, and shal while I may dure
>
> *NPT* 3094. Men dreme of thyng that nevere was ne shal

When the construction includes a subject complement coming later in the sentence, the infinitive is expressed so as to avoid the anacoluthic effect of 'I am, and ever shall, yours':

> *Tr* I.988. Wherfore I am, and wol ben, ay redy
>
> *Tr* V.152. I am, and shal ben ay, / God helpe me so, while that my lyf may dure, / Youre owene aboven every creature

Other omissions of the infinitive belong to the type 'I have been/done, and shall (be/do)', which is occasionally found in OE. and becomes quite common in ME. (see Visser, pp. 1847–9):

> *HSynne* 12550. þe synne þat y haue do, and more shal
>
> *Tr* III.1326. Yet have I seyd, and God toforn, and shal
>
> *Tr* III.1459. For many a lovere hastow slayn, and wilt
>
> *Tr* V.1317. Righte fresshe flour, whos I ben have and shal
>
> *ClT* 645. 'I have,' quod she, 'seyd thus, and evere shal'
>
> *CYT* 985. Ful many a man hath he bigiled er this, / And wole, if that he lyve may a while

It is of interest that on the odd occasion when Chaucer uses *will* rather than *shall* it is in a depreciatory context: Troilus denounces the day in *Tr* III.1459, and the Canon's Yeoman his master in *CYT* 986. In both instances the auxiliary verb connotes wilful persistence in an unwelcome practice. For expression of the infinitive compare

> *Havelok* 2420. Ich haue you fed, and yet shal fede
>
> *LGW* 1161. Whi I have told this story, and telle shal

Ellipsis also occurs in passive constructions, where both the infinitive of *be* and a past participle are omitted:

> *CMundi* F 17025. Then eny man that euyr was born / or yet shalle of wyve
>
> *Lady* 80. That bettre loved is noon, ne never shal

Tr II.45. For to this purpos this may liken the, / And the right
nought, yet al is seid or schal

Ellipsis of the infinitive rarely occurs in the ME. romances, and for
earlier parallels to Chaucer's usage in his love poetry it would seem that
we must turn to religious and moral writings. The omission of past
participles, on the other hand, is seldom attested before Chaucer and his
contemporaries, and even in the late fourteenth century is of only
sporadic occurrence. Apart from an isolated instance in OE., Visser's
earliest illustration of the type 'I love you, and always have' (p. 1845),
which is so common in modern usage, comes from Langland: *PP* C
XI.18 'he soiourneth with ous freres, / And ay hath, as ich hope'.
Chaucer prefers to express the past participle either of the main verb, as
in *LGW* 2533 '"To God," quod she, "prey I, and ofte have prayed"', or of
the verb *do* used in its vicarious function:

Lady 78. For bothe I love and eek drede yow so soore, / And algates
moot, and have done yow, ful yore

ClT 106. For certes, lord, so wel us liketh yow / And al youre werk,
and evere han doon

The repetition of the object-pronoun in the first example is peculiar, and
may reflect either deliberate emphasis or metrical necessity.

Visser (pp. 1851–2) gives examples of the type 'I shall love you, and
always have' from the mid-fifteenth century onwards, though in most of
them the ellipsis occurs either in a subordinate clause or in a new
sentence altogether. Chaucer uses the construction at least once in his
poetry, in a subordinate clause: *Tr* II.244 'As in my gylt I shal yow
nevere offende; / And if I have er this, I wol amende'. It is understand-
able that the co-ordinate form of expression has been avoided in literary
usage, since the tense-progression from future to perfect is anti-
climactic.

Whereas the infinitive tends to be omitted in the second of two co-
ordinate verb phrases, ellipsis of the past participle occurs in the first in
Chaucer's poetry. Relative clauses of the type 'that have (been) or are
alive' are occasionally met with:

Tr II.888. For alle the folk that han or ben on lyve

Tr V.269. Naught alle the men that han or ben on lyve

Sentences like 'I have (been) and shall be yours' also occur, again in
Troilus and Criseyde, in protestations of romantic fidelity:

CA II.2790. It hath and schal ben everemor

Tr II.827. O Love, to whom I have and shal / Ben humble subgit

Tr III.999. And I, emforth my connyng and my might, / Have and
ay shal, how sore that me smerte, / Ben to yow trewe and hool
with al myn herte

This is a form of syllepsis, in which the two auxiliaries share a main verb that is construed with only one of them. The effect of the construction is not jarring, since in ME. the form *ben* does service for both the infinitive and past participle of the copula. This usage is first recorded in Chaucer's poetry (see Visser, pp. 1852–3). In the fifteenth century the construction was extended to other infinitives, as in a rather grating line from Pecok's *Donet*: 'Y haue and schal eche of þilke conclusions sette forþ'. Such sentences, found in both formal and informal prose, do not appear to have outlived the century.

Visser in his discussion of this form of syllepsis formulates a rule of usage: 'When two or more non-congenerous auxiliaries precede a common verbal complement, the form of this complement is determined by the last of the auxiliaries' (p. 1854). Most of the available evidence supports this rule, which is yet another manifestation of the tendency in English to make agreement depend on proximity. But there is at least one interesting exception in Chaucer's poetry: *Tr* I.593 'I have, and shal, for trewe or fals report, / In wrong and right iloved the al my lyve'. Here it is the first auxiliary, not the second, that determines the form of the main verb; the ellipsis is of an infinitive, though it could hardly be expressed in this position. The construction testifies to the independent character of 'and shal', which normally occurs at the end of a clause but is used by Pandarus, as little more than a polite tag, near the beginning. In attempting to convince Troilus that he is to be trusted with his secret, Pandarus recognises that the appeal is more likely to be successful if his profession of friendship refers primarily to past performance and secondarily, as a matter of courtesy, to the future.

It is perhaps not surprising that infinitives should be more commonly omitted than past participles in Chaucer's poetry, considering the partiality of ME. writers for the broken order of words. The ellipsis of a co-ordinate past participle is a suspensive construction that looks forward to a main verb later in the sentence, whereas the ellipsis of an infinitive normally occurs after the main verb has been expressed and the sentence has thus achieved a completeness that accommodates the addition of elliptical material. The omission of infinitives is often comparable in rhythm and structure to forms of broken order, as the following pairs of constructions illustrate:

Tr I.838. Ne al the men that riden konne or go

Tr V.1317. Righte fresshe flour, whos I ben have and shal

Tr III.1767. To cerclen hertes alle, and faste bynde

Lady 80. That bettre loved is noon, ne never shal

KnT 1362. That lene he wex and drye as is a shaft

Tr IV.1680. That I as youre, and shal whil I may dure

CHAPTER VI

Relative Clauses

Certain features of word-order and sentence-structure that have been discussed in the preceding chapters are to be seen in Chaucer's relative clauses, which assume a variety of forms and positions in his poetry. Here we shall consider the postponement of relative clauses, their reinforcement by means of personal pronouns, the ellipsis of relative pronouns, and the place of prepositions in these clauses and in related infinitive constructions. These are matters which have a direct bearing on the study of syntax and style, for the relative clause represents one of the commonest forms of subordination in the language, and in its various guises may be used for purposes beyond the purely grammatical function of qualifying an antecedent noun or pronoun. Some attention is given to stylistic functions in an early monograph on Chaucer's relative constructions by L. R. Wilson, which provides a full outline that may still be consulted with profit. The object of the present chapter is rather to establish a few main points of usage, at least one of which has not previously been given sufficient notice as a characteristic feature of ME. syntax and style.

1 POSTPONEMENT

One of the most frequent forms of discontinuous modification in ME. is the separation of a relative clause from its antecedent. This illustrates a general tendency of English in all periods 'to reserve the final position for the more complex parts of a clause or sentence—the principle of end-weight' (Quirk and Greenbaum, p. 410), and in ME. it is yet another example of the lack of suspensiveness that we have often observed in other areas of syntax. While such constructions seldom cause serious ambiguity, many instances would now be regarded as illogical misplacements. In *Gowther* 470 'He feld tho baner in tho feld, / That schon so bryght and schene' it is the banner that shone brightly, not the field; the context normally enables us to identify the correct antecendent. Postponement is common to all forms and styles of ME. poetry:

> *Havelok* 1718. And Goldeboru shal ete with me, / þat is so fayr so
> flour on tre
>
> *HSynne* 9201. þe fyrst man was þe fadyr, þe prest, / þat deyd aftye þe
> doȝtyr nest
>
> *Launfal* 443. þe lordes ryden out arowe / þat were yn þat castell
>
> *Patience* 373. Heter hayreȝ þay hent þat asperly bited
>
> *HF* 520. And ye, me to endite and ryme / Helpeth, that on Parnaso
> duelle
>
> *Tr* II.100. This romaunce is of Thebes that we rede
>
> *Tr* III.370. How dorst I mo tellen of this matere, / That quake now?
>
> *GenProl* 9. And smale foweles maken melodye, / That slepen al the
> nyght with open ye
>
> *KnT* 1110. Of oure lynage have som compassioun, / That is so lowe
> ybroght by tirannye
>
> *MLT* 890. The hand was knowe that the lettre wroot
>
> *SumT* 1754. A sturdy harlot wente ay hem bihynde, / That was hir
> hostes man
>
> *PardT* 766. God save yow, that boghte agayn mankynde
>
> *MkT* 2231. This hand was sent from God that on the wal / Wroot
> *Mane, techel, phares*, truste me
>
> *SecNT* 290. And she gan kisse his brest, that herde this

Postponed relative clauses may be used for special effect. As we have seen, the construction in *HF* 520-1 serves with other forms of discontinuity, all of them well-established in ME. usage, 'to produce a "difficult" effect reminiscent of Dante and Latin poetry' (Burrow 1971, p. 22).

Discontinuity is also a normal feature of certain stereotyped forms of expression:

> *Havelok* 957. Alle him loueden þat him sowen
>
> *MLT* 532. That alle hir loven that looken in hir face
>
> *ClT* 413. That ech hire lovede that looked in hir face

and of expansions of sentences like 'The time is come':

> *Tr* IV.914. Syn wel ye woot the tyme is faste by, / That he shal come
>
> *WBT* 988. That day was come that homward moste he tourne
>
> *MerchT* 1768. The tyme cam that resoun was to ryse

The following examples, however, exhibit a peculiarity of alliterative usage, and have no exact parallels in Chaucer's poetry:

GGK 428. þe blod brayd fro þe body, þat blykked on þe grene

GGK 2003. þe snawe snitered ful snart, þat snayped þe wylde

These relative clauses do not so much define the antecedent as present a consequence of the action in the principal clause. In Chaucer's usage it would be normal to link the clauses by means of *and*.

C. T. Onions notes that in modern literary usage 'a possessive adjective or pronoun has sometimes a relative depending on it; in such circumstances *my (mine)*, *his*, *their (theirs)*, &c. are mentally analysed as equivalent to *of me*, *of him*, *of them*, &c.' (p. 136). This necessarily discontinuous construction is of common occurrence in ME. poetry:

Havelok 1256. And saw it comen ut of his mouth, / þat lay bi hire in þe bed

Patience 233. þenne þaȝ her takel were torne þat totered on yþes

HF 1079. And hath so verray hys lyknesse / That spak the word

Tr II.338. That of his deth yow liste noughte to recche, / That is so trewe and worthi, as ye se

WBProl 326. Of alle men his wysedom is the hyeste / That rekketh nevere who hath the world in honde

PardT 649. That vengeance shal nat parten from his hous / That of his othes is to outrageous

There is normally contact between the relative pronoun and the noun qualified by the antecedent possessive adjective; but in *Tr* II.338–9 and *WBProl* 326–7 more extensive separations are found according to the principle of end-weight. The equivalent periphrastic construction is to be seen in *GenProl* 301 'And bisily gan for the soules preye / Of hem that yaf hym wherwith to scoleye'. Postponement also occurs when a possessive adjective is used in the objective relation, as in stereotyped expressions of the following kind:

Amis 302. For his loue, þat bar þe croun of þorn

Isumbras 233. For his love that dyed on rode

Tr II.500. For his love, which that us bothe made

MerchT 2334. Help, for hir love that is of hevene queene

SecNT 138. And, for his love that dyde upon a tree

One form of the postponed relative construction is of particular interest. Donald Davie in his discussion of how syntax can mime a pattern of action in the world at large draws attention to sentences containing a plot in miniature:

The easiest 'plot' to distinguish is the potentially tragic one of 'time brings in his revenges':

And Time that gave doth now his gift confound.

In this Shakespearean line the syntax is unremarkable. There is no tragic reversal on the relative pronoun as in the line from Sackville ['banisht by them whom he did thus detbind'], or in this, from Cowper, on the poplars felled:

> And the tree is my seat that once lent me a shade . . . (p. 80)

Here the postponement of the relative clause exploits a lack of suspensiveness in effecting a reversal of the normal time-sequence. The construction also occurs several times in ME. poetry:

Amis 1540. & his broþer, Sir Amiloun, / Wiþ sorwe & care was driuen adoun, / þat ere was hende & fre

Purity 1685. þus he countes hym a kow, þat watȝ a kyng ryche

Patience 296. Now he knaweȝ hym in care þat couþe not in sele

Tr I.507. He sayde, 'O fool, now artow in the snare, / That whilom japedest at loves peyne'

Tr IV.313. Syn she is queynt, that wont was yow to lighte

Tr V.546. Syn she is went that wont was us to gye

A. C. Spearing has shown how postponed relative clauses in *Purity* help to evoke 'a world in which sudden reversals of fortune are the common order of things' (1970, p. 70). It is fitting that in Chaucer's poetry it should be Troilus who gives expression to the notion of ironic reversal by means of this construction; in the midst of his self-conscious rhetorical gestures it captures exactly the perception of a world subject to the sudden and contrary operation of forces beyond his control. One might feel that the construction would commend itself to the Monk, but his relentless cataloguing of Fortune's victims preserves chronology and leaves little room for irony.

II REINFORCEMENT

Before and during the development of the interrogative pronouns *who*, *whom*, and *whose* as relatives in the ME. period, it was a common practice to indicate these functions by attaching a personal pronoun to indeclinable relatives such as *that*. Here first are some examples of the reinforced construction in which there is contact between *that* and a personal subject-pronoun:

Arthour A 339. No miȝt þer askaþe neuer on / þat he nas to deþ ydon

Havelok 2159. Was non of hem þat he ne gret

BD 693. For there nys planete in firmament, / Ne in ayr ne in erthe noon element, / That they ne yive me a yifte echone / Of wepynge

Tr II.777. Ther loveth noon, that she nath why to pleyne

LGW 1260. Where sen ye oon, that he ne hath laft his leef?

KnT 2843. 'Right as ther dyed nevere man,' quod he, / 'That he ne lyvede in erthe in some degree, / Right so ther lyvede never man,' he seyde, / 'In al this world, that som tyme he ne deyde'

MillT 3110. In al the route nas ther yong ne oold / That he ne seyde it was a noble storie

MkT 2330. That ther nas kyng ne prynce in al that lond / That he nas glad, if that he grace fond

Malory 593/16. they founde nother man nother woman that he ne was dede

This is by far the commonest form of reinforcement in ME. Visser in his account of it expresses the widely-held view that, in both Old and Middle English usage, 'the task of *he* in the *þat he* type was mainly to accentuate the subject character of the invariable relatives *þat* and *þe*' (p. 58). But this does not explain why the nominative form *þe he* should seldom if ever occur in OE., or why *that he* in ME. should be found more often than the oblique forms *that him* and *that his*, where the particle is in greater need of pronominal reinforcement.

Two essential features of reinforced relative clauses are often overlooked. The first is that they normally occur in negative sentences, particularly in the nominative and objective forms. Negation is emphatic, and emphasis invites redundancy of expression. The pleonastic personal pronoun may therefore be seen to supply a further measure of emphasis in negative sentences; in verse it serves also as a metrical convenience, in taking a heavy stress before the unemphatic particle *ne*. The second and more important feature of reinforced relative clauses is their close resemblance to consecutive clauses, as the following sentences illustrate:

Havelok 949. It was non so litel knaue, / For to leyken, ne forto plawe, / þat he nolde with him pleye

RvT 3937. Ther dorste no wight hand upon hym legge, / That he ne swoor he sholde anon abegge

SumT 2178. That in this world is noon so povre a page / That he nolde have abhomynacioun

In such sentences the ambiguity of the clause introduced by *that he* is often to be resolved only by reference to the context. Visser (p. 59) finds a relative clause in the first example, and so must take the sentence to mean 'There was no little boy who would not play with Havelok'; but the more probable sense is 'There was no boy so little that Havelok would not play with him', which provides further touching evidence of the hero's good nature. Although here, as often, the presence of *so* in the principal clause points forward to a consecutive clause, the expression of this particle was not a fixed requirement in ME.; *RvT* 3937–8 is an example of an unheralded consecutive construction, with *that* being equivalent to 'such that'. On the other hand, *so* is sometimes followed

107

later by an ordinary relative clause: *HarlLyr* 4.26 'In world nis non so wyter mon / þat al hire bounte telle con'. Just how close relative and consecutive constructions can be in ME. is suggested by sentences like that in *SumT* 2178–9, where either analysis yields a satisfactory sense.

Erich Auerbach has observed of the medieval European languages in general that

> in the slow growth of a hypotactically richer and more periodic syntax, a leading role seems to have been played (down to the time of Dante) by consecutive constructions . . . . While other types of modal connection were still comparatively undeveloped, this one flourished and developed characteristic functions of expressions which were later lost. (p. 128)

The truth of this remark is borne out by examination of the ME. rhyming romances, where the consecutive clause is a characteristic device of emphatic expression; in *Havelok*, for example, instances will be found on almost every page. It therefore seems likely that, with the replacement of þe by *that* as a relative particle, the opportunity was taken to exploit the ambiguous character of the latter form in its collocation with personal pronouns. The primary function of the pleonastic subject-pronoun is not so much 'to accentuate the subject character of the invariable relatives' as to give the construction a measure of consecutive force in emphatic negative sentences, which accounts for the absence of the form þe he in OE. writings.

The earliest reinforced relative clauses in the subjective relation show contact between *that* and a personal pronoun. The separation of these elements appears to have been a later development in positive sentences, and serves in the main to reinforce the structure of a relative clause without giving it any particular emphasis:

Amis 207. A douhti kniȝt at cri, / þat euer he proued wiþ niþe & ond / For to haue brouȝt hem boþe to schond

Tr I.810. What! many a man hath love ful deere ybought / Twenty wynter that his lady wiste, / That nevere yet his lady mouth he kiste

Genprol 43. A knyght ther was, and that a worthy man, / That fro the tyme he first bigan / To riden out, he loved chivalrie

Malory 84/7. Now turne we unto Accalon of Gaule, that whan he awoke he founde hymself by a depe welles syde

Reinforced relative clauses of this type, which tend to be non-restrictive, occur with some frequency in fifteenth-century writings, but only occasionally in Chaucer's poetry. Reinforcement is also found with the relative pronoun *which*, again towards the end of the ME. period (see Visser, p. 59).

It is usual for the elements to be separated in reinforced relative clauses in the objective relation, since the normal place for a personal object-pronoun is after the verb. Although they are less frequently met with in Chaucer's poetry, such clauses also occur mainly in emphatic negative sentences and are related to consecutive constructions. The following list includes examples of both direct and indirect objects:

> GGK 2104. þer passes non bi þat place so proude in his armes / þat he ne dyngez hym to depe with dynt of his honde

> Anel 113. Ther nas to her no maner lettre sent / That touched love, from any maner wyght, / That she ne shewed hit him

> Tr V.114. That ther nas thyng with which he myghte hire plese, / That he nolde don his peyne and al his myght / To don it

> LGW 1114. There nas courser wel ybrydeled non . . . That in the lan of Libie may be gete, / That Dido ne hath it Eneas ysent

> KnT 1897. For in the lond ther was no crafty man / That geometrie or ars-metrike kan, / Ne portreyour, ne kervere of ymages, / That Theseus ne yaf him mete and wages

It will be noticed that in each of the examples from Chaucer the re-inforced relative clause follows a normal restrictive relative clause. For the expression of a pleonastic object-pronoun after the second of two co-ordinate verbs, see GenProl 550 'Ther was no dore that he nolde heve of harre, / Or breke it at a rennyng with his heed'. This occurs also in one instance of Chaucer's infrequent use of the objective construction in its positive form:

> CMundi C 15995. þis it was þat ilk cok, / þat petre herd him crau

> MillT 3429. I saugh to-day a cors yborn to chirche / That now on Monday last, I saw hym wirche

> MkT 2649. Of kynges, princes, dukes, erles bolde / Whiche he conquered, and broghte hem into wo

Lastly, there is the reinforcement of a relative pronoun by a possessive adjective, usually his:

> Havelok 1808. Was non of hem þat hise hernes / Ne lay þer-ute ageyn þe sternes

> Havelok 1855. For was þer non, long ne lite, / þat he mouhte ouer-take, / þat he ne garte his croune krake

> ABC 161. Xristus, thi sone, that in this world alighte / Upon the cros to suffre his passioun, / And eek that Longius his herte pighte

> HF 76. That alwey for to slepe hir wone is

> Tr II.318. Which alwey for to don wel is his wone

> KnT 2710. That with a spere was thirled his brest boon

> SqT 149. There is no fowel that fleeth under the hevene / That she ne shal wel understonde his stevene

> PrT 504. That day by day to scole was his wone

109

Although this has been described as a 'rather clumsy construction' (Brook, p. 155), it offers a useful alternative to relative clauses introduced by *whose* when there is occasion to depart from the normal order of words. In *KnT* 2710, for example, it enables the subject of the relative clause to be placed in a position of greater emphasis. But Chaucer rarely uses the construction in negative sentences, and seems to have regarded it as an occasional convenience, notably in conjunction with the noun *wone.* *This whole chapter is insensitive*

III ELLIPSIS

> Probably no other single question of English syntax has attracted so much attention as that of the omission of the relative pronoun. The term 'omission' requires some qualification; while it is convenient, and even unavoidable, to speak of the omission of the relative pronoun, no relative pronoun has in fact been omitted. The speaker feels no sense of an elided or omitted particle, and the history of the construction is against any theory of omission. (Phillipps, p. 323)

Whatever the history of the construction may be—and it is one for which there is little evidence from before the thirteenth century—the term 'omission' is more than simply a convenience when we are considering the usage of individual authors. In view of the variation in the form of the relative clauses in such sentences as the following, it is questionable whether 'the speaker feels no sense of an elided or omitted particle':

Havelok 907. Wel is set þe mete ʌ þu etes, / And þe hire *þat* þu getes

KnT 2402. Thanne help me, lord, tomorwe in my bataille, / For thilke fyr *that* whilom brente thee, / As wel as thilke fyr ʌ now brenneth me

Of course, some asyndetic clauses may be accounted for by the principle of *apo koinou*, whereby an element common to both clauses is simply not repeated, as in 'There is *somebody* wants to see you'. There are also clauses in which it is a personal pronoun that is omitted:

> Many of the cases usually interpreted as non-expressions of the relative pronoun might equally well be taken as non-expressions of the personal pronoun, as in *I fonde þe freris, alle þe foure ordres, Preched þe peple* (PPl. B Prol. 59). In *he sente after a cherle was in the toun* (Ch. CT C Ph. 140), however, *was in the toun* is more likely to be a non-introduced relative clause than a co-ordinate clause. (Mustanoja, p. 205)

In other words, the clause in the first example is non-restrictive and in the second restrictive, a distinction that is usually apparent from the context. The general assertion that the form of the asyndetic relative clause 'is often best explained in terms of omitted personal pronouns rather than omitted relative pronouns' (Phillipps, p. 329) must therefore be treated with caution, since it applies to the special case of headless non-restrictive clauses; in the majority of asyndetic relative clauses it is not possible to insert a personal pronoun.

It may be noted that, while clauses of the type illustrated by the example from *Piers Plowman* are fairly common in ME. alliterative poetry and the rhyming romances, they are seldom used by Chaucer, who prefers to introduce a non-restrictive clause by means of either a relative pronoun, or, occasionally, the co-ordinating conjunction *and*. Compare the following similar sentences, in the first of which a personal pronoun is omitted in a non-restrictive clause, and in the second, a relative pronoun in a restrictive clause:

> *GenProl* 477. A good man was ther of religoun, / And ∧ was a povre persoun of a toun
>
> *GenProl* 529. With hym ther was a plowman, ∧ was his brother, / That hadde ylad of dong ful many a fother

That a relative and not a personal pronoun has been omitted in the second example is clear from the fact that, as is often the case, the asyndetic clause is followed by a normal relative clause. The editorial use of a comma to mark the ellipsis is unnecessary and possibly misleading, and the punctuation of the following examples has been altered accordingly.

Subject-Pronouns

Ellipsis of the relative pronoun is a common feature of present-day spoken English, and in earlier periods it is also found extensively in literary usage. The construction is now most frequent in the objective relation, but in ME. and early MnE. relative subject-pronouns are equally often omitted. The latter form of ellipsis will be considered first, and the major varieties described with reference to the function of the antecedent of the asyndetic clause. Although it is not strictly accurate to say that 'this phenomenon is first seen in texts of the latter half of the 14th century' (Mustanoja, p. 204), it was at this time that the construction came to be widely represented in poetic usage.

1. The antecedent is the subject or complement in an existential clause introduced by *there* or *it*:

> *BD* 160. Save ther were a fewe welles / ∧ Came rennynge fro the clyves adoun
>
> *BD* 674. Ther be but fewe ∧ kan hir begile
>
> *Tr* II.1368. It is oon of the thynges ∧ forthereth most

No evidence is presented for this statement

GenProl 529. With hym ther was a plowman ʌ was his brother

MillT 3190. With hym ther was dwellynge a poure scoler / ʌ Hadde lerned art

CYT 972. Ther is a chanoun of religioun / Amonges us ʌ wolde infecte al a toun

This construction is still in use, especially in dialects; but Chaucer does not often use it in its positive form, nor are there many instances in earlier writings (see Visser, p. 12). It occurs more frequently in ME. in negative sentences, where the antecedent is a negative pronoun or a noun premodified by *no*, as in *Rom* 1239 'For ther is no cloth ʌ sitteth bet / On damysell, than doth roket'. This is Visser's only example (p. 13) from before the fifteenth century, but the construction is found several times in Chaucer's poetry and even earlier in the ME. period:

Amis 869. In al þe court was þer no wiȝt / ʌ Sir Amis borwe durst ben

Isumbras 437. Ther was no man ʌ withstode his dynte

RelLyr XIV 81.35. þare es nane, I þe hete, / Of al þi kyth ʌ wald slepe þe with

BD 740. But ther is no man alyve her / ʌ Wolde for a fers make this woo

HF 1044. Hyt is nothing ʌ will byten the

Tr I.203. Ther nys nat oon ʌ kan war by other be

Tr III.886. For ther is nothyng ʌ myghte hym bettre plese

Tr V.1088. Ther is non auctour ʌ telleth it, I wene

RvT 3932. Ther was no man, for peril, ʌ dorste hym touche

FranklT 854. Is ther no ship, of so manye as I se, / ʌ Wol bryngen hom my lord?

Although in this form the construction has the force of true *apo koinou*, it may be seen as an emphatic expansion of the equivalent simple sentence, with deletion of the relative pronoun. Further contraction of the expanded form results from ellipsis of the formal subject *there*:

PP B V.362. ʌ Is non so hungri hounde in Hertford schire / ʌ Durst lape of the leuynges

MerchT 1634. 'Thanne is ʌ,' quod he, 'no thyng ʌ may me displese'

Faerie Queene I.vii.27. ʌ Was neuer Ladie ʌ loued dearer day

Richard II II.i.173. In war was ʌ never lion ʌ rag'd more fierce

This worn-down form of expression comes close to the structure of the simple sentence from which it derives. The relationship between these constructions, and others described elsewhere in the present study, may be seen from the following table:

A 1   No thyng may me displese
  2   May no thyng me displese (see p. 16)
  3   Ther may no thyng me displese (p. 18)
B 1 a Ther is no thyng that may me displese
    b Ther is no thyng ∧ may me displese
    c Ther ∧ no thyng ∧ may me displese (p. 17)
  2 a ∧ Is no thyng that may me displese (p. 16)
    b ∧ Is no thyng ∧ may me displese

All of these sentence-patterns occur in Chaucer's poetry, and they offer striking evidence of the variety available to the ME. poet in the negative mode of expression. The range of positive equivalents is small in comparison.

   2. The antecedent is the object of a verb in the principal clause, which Kellner (p. 62) considers a development of *apo koinou* usage in the subjective relation:

> *Amis* 314. [Sir Amiloun] drouʒ forþ tvay coupes of gold / ∧ Ware liche in al þing
>
> *CA* V.4156. And tok a swerd ∧ was of assay
>
> *BD* 365. I asked oon ∧ ladde a lymere
>
> *LGW* 964. He hadde a knyght ∧ was called Achates
>
> *SqT* 316. Ye mooten trille a pyn ∧ stant in his ere
>
> *PhysT* 140. He sente after a cherl ∧ was in the toun
>
> *NPT* 3035. and fond / A dong-carte ∧ wente as it were to donge lond, / That was arrayed in that same wise
>
> *NPT* 3175. For he hadde founde a corn ∧ lay in the yerd

But the principle of *apo koinou* does not always account for the form of such sentences. In *WBProl* 608 'I hadde the beste *quoniam* myghte be', for example, the clause 'the beste *quoniam* myghte be' does not make sense on its own; nor, for the same reason, can the ellipsis be of a personal pronoun. More generally, it is not strictly true to say that 'utterances of the type "I have an uncle is a myghty erle" consist of two syntactical units with one element in common (in this example "an uncle") which functions as the subject in the second unit' (Visser, p. 11), since the use of the indefinite article is appropriate only in the first instance.

   3. The antecedent is the headword of a prepositional phrase in the principal clause:

> *Amis* 772. In at an hole ∧ was nouʒt to wide / He seiʒe hem boþe in þat tide
>
> *Athelston* 16. By a forest gan they mete / Wiþ a cros ∧ stood in a strete
>
> *WedGawen* 246. She satt on a palfray ∧ was gay begon

CA IV.1287. And forth sche wente prively / Unto the Park ⋀ was faste by

BD 1315. Gan homwardes for to ryde / Unto a place ⋀ was there besyde

PF 18. it happede me for to beholde / Upon a bok ⋀ was write with lettres olde

LGW F 510. Hastow nat in a book ⋀ lyth in thy cheste / The grete goodnesse of the quene Alceste?

MerchT 1883. And in a purs of sylk ⋀ heng on his sherte / He hath it put

PardT 664. they herde a belle clynke / Biforn a cors ⋀ was caried to his grave

The construction illustrated here and in the preceding paragraph is often equivalent to other forms of postmodification. If the verb of the asyndetic clause is the copula *be*, the equivalent construction is a postmodifying phrase ('unto a place *there besyde*'); if the verb is either a compound tense formed with a past participle or a finite lexical verb, the equivalent construction is a postmodifying non-finite clause introduced by either a past participle ('upon a bok *write with lettres olde*') or a present participle ('in a purs of sylk *hangynge on his sherte*'). In conveying a more accurate notion of tense than do these forms of postmodification, and in its conciseness, the asyndetic clause often lends a vivid touch to passages of narrative and description.

4. The antecedent is the headword in a phrase or clause introduced by *like* or *as*:

PP B V.82. And as a leke ⋀ hadde yleye longe in the sonne, / So loked he

CA IV.2867. And makth him ded as for a throwe, / Riht as a Stok ⋀ were overthrowe

WBT 1095. Ye faren lyk a man ⋀ had lost his wit

ClT 2. Ye ryde as coy and stille as dooth a mayde / ⋀ Were newe spoused

CYProl 580. His forheed dropped as a stillatorie / ⋀ Were ful of plantayne and of paritorie

In comparisons of this kind, where the verb of the asyndetic clause is in the subjunctive mood, it is once again impossible to find *apo koinou* or the ellipsis of a personal pronoun.

In conclusion, brief mention may be made of one other construction in which the omission of a relative subject-pronoun plays a part, and of one in which it does not. Ellipsis has been carried to an advanced stage in *BD* 181 'whoo ys ⋀ lyth there?', the form of which appears to derive from expansion of the simple question 'whoo lyth there?' into a cleft sentence, 'whoo ys hit that lyth there?', with subsequent deletion of both the relative pronoun and its antecedent. This usage is suggestive of the spoken language; for a similar case of structural erosion compare the presence of a residual copula in sentences like 'Is no man may me displese'. The second point concerns the construction of *FrT* 1524 'I am a yeman, ʌ knowen is ful wyde'. Miss Schlauch (p. 1111) includes the line among her examples of asyndetic relative clauses; but for this to be so, the verb in the second clause would have to be *am* in accordance with a rule of agreement in Early English usage (see Visser, p. 93). The clause is in fact missing a personal or demonstrative subject-pronoun: 'it/that is very widely known'.

Object-Pronouns

The ellipsis of relative object-pronouns can be traced back to OE. and has been in common use since the late ME. period (see Visser, pp. 536ff.), though it is less frequent in Chaucer's poetry than ellipsis in the subjective relation. In this construction the relative pronoun, were it to be expressed, would normally be the object of a verb in the asyndetic clause. Once again, the varieties of the construction to be considered here will be distinguished according to the function of the antecedent in the principal clause.

1. The antecedent is the subject of the principal clause, which often takes the form of an existential clause introduced by *there*:

Havelok 907. Wel is set þe mete ʌ þu etes

Anel 253. Alas! is ther now nother word ne chere / ʌ Ye vouchen sauf upon myn hevynesse?

Tr I.577. Ther is another thing ʌ I take of hede

RvT 3989. And nameliche ther was a greet collegge / ʌ Men clepen the Soler Halle at Cantebregge

WBT 1083. Greet was the wo ʌ the knyght hadde in his thoght

PardT 675. Ther cam a privee theef ʌ men clepeth Deeth

The asyndetic clause normally follows the complete principal clause in Chaucer's poetry; it is less commonly found embedded in the principal clause, as in *LGW* 1987 'the beste red ʌ I can / Is that we do the gayler prively / To come'. In a special form of the construction the asyndetic clause is separated from its antecedent:

LGW 2622. The nyght is come ʌ the bryd shal go to bedde

MLT 414. The tyme cam ʌ this olde Sowdanesse / Ordeyned hath this feeste

MLT 722. The tyme is come ʌ a knave child she beer

Here the omission is of *that* as a subordinating conjunction equivalent to 'when' (see *OED* s.v. rel. pron. 7) and not, as Wilson (p. 42) claims, of a relative pronoun and a preposition. For the full form of the construction see p. 104 above.

2. The antecedent is the object of a verb or preposition in the principal clause:

Orfeo A 263. Lord! who may telle þe sore / ∧ þis king sufferd ten ȝere & more?

GGK 1874. Lays vp þe luf-lace ∧ þe lady hym raȝt

PP B V.607. I parfourned þe penaunce ∧ þe preest me enioyned

HF 911. Seest thou any toun / Or ought ∧ thou knowest yonder doun?

HF 1282. What shuld I make lenger tale / Of alle the peple ∧ y ther say?

PF 462. Take she my lif and al the good ∧ I have

Tr II.95. To herken of youre book ∧ ye preysen thus

Tr III.1720. And held aboute hym alwey, out of dred, / A world of folk, as com hym wel of kynde, / The fresshest and the beste ∧ he koude fynde

Thop 708. For oother tale certes kan I noon, / But of a rym ∧ I lerned longe agoon

The example from *Sir Orfeo* suggests that this is an appropriate place to mention the ellipsis of a relative object-pronoun in exclamatory sentences:

BD 1244. Allas! that day / The sorwe ∧ I suffred, and the woo

HF 1393. But, Lord! the perry and richesse / ∧ I saugh sittyng on this godesse! / And, Lord! the hevenyssh melodye / Of songes, ful of armonye, / ∧ I herde aboute her trone ysonge

WBProl 384. O Lord! the peyne ∧ I dide hem and the wo

3. The antecedent is the headword of an adjunct in the principal clause or in a clause subordinated to it. Here first are some examples of ellipsis after adjuncts of place:

HSynne 9018. þey come to a tounne ∧ men calles Colbek

Amis 22. And in what lond ∧ þei were born

HF 1106. Thou shalt se me go as blyve / Unto the nexte laure ∧ y see

LGW 2481. And hom he goth the nexte wey ∧ he myghte

MillT 3760. A softe paas he wente over the strete / Until a smyth ∧ men cleped daun Gervays

Ellipsis also occurs after adjuncts of manner:

Havelok 2631. With þe swerd ∧ he held ut-drawen

Tr III.1586. To hym to com in al the haste ∧ he may

MLT 346. And everich, in the beste wise ∧ he kan, / To strengthen hire shall alle his frendes fonde

MerchT 1405. For I wol be, certeyn, a wedded man, / And that anoon in al the haste ∧ I kan

After adjuncts of time the omission is once again of the conjunction only, not of a relative pronoun and a preposition:

> *Havelok* 2090. þe firste niht ʌ he lay þer-inne, / Hise wif . . . Wok Ubbe
>
> *HF* 1906. Unto the tyme ʌ y hidder com
>
> *Tr* V.1187. For thilke nyght ʌ I last Criseyde say
>
> *LGW* 1951. Tyl thilke tyme ʌ he sholde freten be
>
> *KnT* 2412. And evermo, unto that day ʌ I dye
>
> *SqT* 476. Unto the tyme ʌ she gan of swough awake

Ellipsis is also found after prepositional phrases of other kinds: a genitive phrase in *Tr* IV.1238 'to han ben crowned queene / Of al the lond ʌ the sonne on shyneth sheene', and a prepositional phrase denoting an abstract relation in *MLT* 846 'Thanne is ther no comparison bitwene / Thy wo and any wo ʌ man may sustene'. Finally, the ellipsis of a relative object-pronoun in constructions of the type 'by the faith ʌ I owe to you' is common in the ME. period (see Visser, pp. 537–8):

> *Havelok* 1666. Bi þe fey ʌ I owe to þe
>
> *CMundi* C 5145. Sir, be þe faith ʌ i haue to yow
>
> *Tr* III.791. And by that feith ʌ I shal Priam of Troie
>
> *Tr* III.1649. And by that feyth ʌ I shal to God and yow
>
> *Rom* 2106. By thilke feith ʌ ye owe to me

A special construction remains to be considered which, though it has the appearance of ellipsis, may be accounted for by the use of *that* as a demonstrative-relative particle representing a phonetically reduced form of OE. *þæt þe* 'that which' (see Visser, pp. 546–9). *What* has gradually replaced *that* in this function in MnE., except in questions, where it would conflict with the same form of the interrogative pronoun. Thus we find 'What is *that* you are doing?', which preserves the earlier usage, beside 'Tell me *what* you are doing'. The demonstrative-relative in sentences of this kind acts as an object to the verb in each of two clauses:

> *Amis* 396. Do al þat þou may
>
> *GGK* 390. Sir Gawan, me lykes / þat I schal fange at þy fust þat I haf frayst here
>
> *HF* 1024. Maistow not heren that I do?
>
> *LGW* F 370. To translaten that olde clerkes writen
>
> *GenProl* 442. He kepte that he wan in pestilence
>
> *WBProl* 781. They haten that hir housbondes loven ay

When *that* is the object of the same preposition in the two clauses, the preposition is often omitted in the relative clause:

Tr I.648. Counseillen the of that thow art amayed ∧

Tr V.1295. To know a soth of that thow art in doute ∧

Rom 2936. Of that thou were in drede and doute ∧

That also functions in ME. as the subject of both the principal clause and a relative clause embedded in it, a construction that Chaucer seems to reserve for the expression of tautologies:

CA I.603. That was a Rose is thanne a thorn

BD 42. That wil not be mot nede be left

BD 708. For that ys doon ys not to come

HF 361. But that is don is not to done

Other constructions are found in which the particle serves in a combination of subjective and objective functions. In the following sentences, for example, *that* is the subject of an embedded relative clause and the object of a verb in the principal clause:

WedGawen 71. And that is amys I shalle amende itt

BD 635. That ys broght up, she set al doun

Another formation, with the appearance of *apo koinou*, has the particle serving as object and subject respectively:

HF 45. That yt forwot that ys to come

HF 118. To make lythe of that was hard

HF 1103. to shewe now / That in myn hed ymarked ys

MerchT 1459. To do al that a man bilongeth to

The fact that these and other examples of demonstrative-relative usage come in the main from Chaucer's early poetry suggests that he found the constructions to be especially suited to the compactness of the octo-syllabic line.

The asyndetic relative clause has an inherent directness, particularly in its now less familiar subjective forms, and may often be used with other features to achieve special effects. Its conciseness is turned to account in the spirited dialogue of *The House of Fame* (see lines 562, 912, 1044, 1107, 1283, 1393-4, 1395-7), and, on a smaller scale, in the description of the hunt in *The Book of the Duchess*:

> Ther overtok y a gret route
> Of huntes and eke of foresteres,
> With many relayes and lymeres,
> And ∧ hyed hem to the forest faste
> And I ∧ with hem. So at the laste
> I asked oon ∧ ladde a lymere:
> 'Say, felowe, who shal hunte here?'

Quod I, and he answered ageyn,
'Syr, th'emperour Octovyen,'
Quod he, 'and ʌ ys here faste by.'
'A Goddes half, in good tyme!' quod I,
'Go we faste!' and ʌ gan to ryde. (360–71)

Wolfgan Clemen in his discussion of the poem refers to 'elliptical phrases where the relative is omitted, "swallowed" as it were, in the hasty and emotional pressure of the narrative' (p. 62). Here the ellipsis in line 365 combines with the omission of personal pronouns (lines 363, 369, 371) and a verb of motion (line 364) to enact the speed with which events occur. These omissions are of a piece with the rapid exchange of dialogue in conveying an impression of urgency in the narrator's penetration of his dream-world.

IV THE PLACE OF PREPOSITIONS

ME. usage was flexible in the placing of prepositions in relative clauses in the objective relation. A preposition might precede the relative pronoun or come after or before the verb. This last is the normal order of words in OE., and it is also frequently met with in ME. poetry:

Arthour L 637. Anon þeo feond þat y of tolde

Havelok 2105. Bi Crist, þat alle folk on leues

HSynne 9019. þe cherche of þe tounne þat þey to come

Launfal 752. And cursede þe mouþ þat he wyth spek

HF 77. And to this god, that I of rede

Tr III.32. Of thynges, which that folk on wondren so

LGW 2385. That nevere harm agilte ne deserved / Unto this crewel man, that she of wiste

MLT 1020. but fader hath he noon / That I of woot

Visser observes that pre-verb order 'held its ground until about the middle of the thirteenth century, when it began to be superseded by the type illustrated in §410 ("That I believe on"), and only remained in use in poetry, apparently to meet the requirements of rime and metre' (pp. 399–400). Post-verb order is attested from early ME. onwards:

HSynne 9022. Seynt Magnes suster, þat þey come to

Isumbras 118. All the sorow that we ben inne

PP B V.603. Of Almes-dedes ar the hokes that the gates hangen on

HF 1894. But these be no such tydynges / As I mene of

Tr II.6. Of disespeir that Troilus was inne

Tr III.513. Right for the fyn that I shal speke of here

SqT 578. Out of that place which that I was inne

CYProl 562. The hors eek that his yeman rood upon

CYT 763. Biforn thise poudres that I speke of heer

This is the normal order of words when the verb of the relative clause is the copula *be*, which gives a sense of incompleteness in end position. Pleonastic constructions such as that in *GenProl* 41 'And eek in what array that that they were inne' illustrate the use of prepositional re-inforcement when post-verb order is preferred with the copula.

A restriction on the placing of prepositions in relative clauses intro-duced by *that* or *as* is that they cannot generally precede the relative pronoun, except, as we have seen, when *that* is used as a demonstrative-relative equivalent to 'that which'. A preposition does come before *that* in *Rom* 3040 'But Resoun conceyved of a sighte / Shame, of that I spak aforn', and this exceptional usage may be taken as further evidence that Fragment B of the translation, at least in the form in which it has come down to us, is not by Chaucer. When the relative pronoun is *whom* or *which*, it has been possible since early ME. to place the preposition either after the verb or before the relative pronoun (see Visser, p. 401). Chaucer normally uses the latter order of words:

Arthour A 665. Ac þe deuelen of whom y said

Arthour A 677. Bi whom he hadde a sone fre

HF 969. All the wey thrugh which I cam

KnT 893. This duc, of whom I make mencioun

MillT 3127. With which I wol now quite the Knyghtes tale

SqT 18. He kepte his lay, to which that he was sworn

SqT 359. That causeth dreem of which ther nys no charge

Post-verb order occurs less frequently:

MLT 984. But to kyng Alla, which I spak of yoore

MancT 78. Yet hadde I levere payen for the mare / Which he rit on

Prepositions may occur in either of two positions in relation to an object in the relative clause. It is usual in Chaucer's poetry for the pre-position to be placed after the object:

Havelok 2752. þat he smot **him with** so sore

Octavian 251. What dethe that ye wyll put me tyll

WBProl 369. That ye may likne youre parables to

CYT 880. Which that they myghte wrappe hem inne a-nyght

This has long been the standard pattern of usage, but occasionally the preposition comes between the verb and its object:

HF 1938. Swiche as men to these cages thwite, / Or maken of these panyers

Tr I.577. Ther is another thing I take of hede

The place of prepositions in relative clauses may be compared with their place in infinitive clauses used to qualify nouns and adjectives (see Visser, p. 405). When an infinitive clause construed with a preposition serves as an adjunct to an adjective, the normal order in Early English is adjective + preposition + infinitive:

Alisaunder L 541. Swiþe grisly on to seon

BD 1177. That is so semely on to see

LGW 2425. Ligurges doughter, fayrer on to sene / Than is the flour ageyn the bryghte sonne

KnT 1082. That art so pale and deedly on to see

MillT 3247. She was ful moore blisful on to see

Post-infinitive order is found less often in such expressions, as in *Isumbras* 251 'Here lere bryghte to se upon'. The same variation in word-order obtains in ME. when the infinitive clause is used to post-modify a noun. In the older form of construction the preposition comes between the noun and the infinitive:

Amis 1760. Sende me so michel of al mi gode, / An asse, on to ride

Patience 199. Hatʒ þou, gome, no gouernour ne god on to calle?

PF 168. I shal the shewe mater of to wryte

Tr II.404. And sende yow than a myrour in to prye

Tr II.1274. God sende mo swich thornes on to pike

Post-infinitive order occurs as early as the twelfth century, possibly under ON. influence, and is commonly found in Chaucer's poetry:

Havelok 864. Ne hauede he no frend to gangen til

Amis 1772. Sende him so michel of al his gode / As an asse to riden opon

PP B VII.129. Haue thei no gernere to go to

PF 695. I wok, and others bokes tok me to, / To reede upon

Tr III.657. This were a weder for to slepen inne

WBProl 573. That hath but oon hole for to sterte to

CYT 881. And a brat to walken inne by daylyght

Prosodic considerations no doubt played a part in the choice of construction; but with *to* postposition was necessary so as to avoid juxtaposing the particle in two different functions. The juxtaposition in *PF* 695–6 is for another reason, and straddles two lines of verse.

When the infinitive takes an object, the preposition has two possible positions in ME. More commonly met with is the order infinitive + preposition + object:

Havelok 782. And hemp to maken of gode lines

PP B VI.297. And profred Peres this present to plese with hunger

CA I.248. To reule with thi conscience

MandTravels 8/19. oyle of mercy for to anoynte with his membres

HF 1133. To bilden on a place hye

Tr IV.426. T'abbrege with thi bittre peynes smerte

GenProl 791. That ech of yow, to shorte with oure weye

MillT 3119. Somwhat to quite with the Knyghtes tale

PardProl 345. To saffron with my predicacioun

ShipT 273. To store with a place that is oures

CYT 1055. Somwhat to quyte with youre kyndenesse

KQuair 777. In this mater to schorten with thy sore

This construction is often equivalent to a relative clause introduced by a preposition: with the form of expression in *MillT* 3119 compare the Miller's declaration a few lines later that he has a story 'With which I wol now quite the Knyghtes tale' (3127). Most instances are found with the preposition *with*, which is seen to have 'a more or less vague reference to some thing or circumstance by means of which the action of the infinitive takes place' (Kenyon, p. 34).

The modern form of the construction, with the preposition coming after the object, occurs less often in ME. writings:

Havelok 760. Gode paniers dede he make, / On til him, and oþer þrinne / Til hise sones, to beren fish inne

PP B VI.149. And of my catel to cope hem with

HF 1141. Any lettres for to rede / Hir names by

MkT 2745. And Phebus eek a fair towaille hym broughte / To dryen hym with

This word-order tends to be used with pronominal objects. The construction is not to be confused with another of similar form, as in *CYT* 1163 'and stopped was, withouten faille, / This hole with wex, to kepe the lemaille in', where *in* is used as an adverb with an infinitive of purpose (= 'in order to keep the filings inside'). It may also be noted that other arrangements of the construction are to be found in the poetry of Chaucer's contemporaries:

Emaré 824. And fylled hem fulle of wordes wele, / Hys men mery wyth to make

GGK 2223. A denez ax nwe dyȝt, þe dynt with to ȝelde

The object of the infinitive has been thrown into front position in both examples, with the addition of a predicate adjective in the first, so as to effect a complete inversion of the usual ME. order.

It is now possible to compare the places of prepositions in relative and infinitive clauses containing an object. The preposition in type A comes after, and in type B before, the object:

A 1 That he smote the man with —
  2 To smite the man with

B 1 That he smote with the man
  2 To smite with the man —

We might expect from this that one type would represent the normal pattern of usage. It has been shown, however, that A1 and B2 predominate over A2 and B1 in Chaucer's poetry; that is, he preferred the modern form of construction in relative clauses and the older form in infinitive clauses.

No statistics to let us know how much more frequent either construction is.

CHAPTER VII

Co-ordination and Parataxis

Some idiomatic functions of *and* in Chaucer's poetry have been described in Chapter 3, and there has been occasional reference elsewhere to its use as a co-ordinating conjunction. The purpose of this final chapter is to consider forms of co-ordination and parataxis in which *and* is or is not expressed. Chaucer's use of conjunctions has received attention in an early monograph by Hermann Eitle, and there is a more general study of co-ordinate expressions in ME. by Urban Ohlander (1936) which provides material for the background to Chaucer's usage. In the following outline, particular reference will be made to constructions which are relevant to the study of syntax and style. It should be noted that the attention here given to co-ordination and parataxis is not meant to imply that they are the most typical features of Chaucer's sentence-structure, or to support the claim that 'in medieval English it was difficult to make up complex sentences with many subordinate clauses' (Blake, p. 144). *What is the purpose?*

I CO-ORDINATION

The simplest method of constructing sentences of more than one clause is the linking of clauses by means of *and*. The serial method of construction is found in all periods of the language, though it is now considered archaic or unsophisticated if indulged in too freely. Certain types of early prose, from the *Anglo-Saxon Chronicle* to Malory's *Morte Darthur*, are built up on this pattern, which is no doubt most widely familiar from the Authorised Version of the Bible:

And Abraham ran unto the herd, and fetcht a calf tender and good, and gave it unto a young man; and he hasted to dress it. And he took butter, and milk, and the calf which he had dressed, and set it before them; and he stood by them under the tree, and they did eat. (Gen. xviii.7–8)

But even in this simply constructed passage *and* does not consistently indicate the same logical relationship between the clauses; as Kellner observes, 'it is scarcely possible to connect sentences together without a certain kind of *hypotaxis* or subordination' (p. 52). For the purpose of description, however, a purely co-ordinative relation may be assumed to exist. Quirk and Greenbaum (p. 257) recognise eight 'semantic implications of coordination by *and*' in contemporary English, and these can be seen to fall into three categories: (i) the normal relation (pure addition); (ii) the adversative relation; and (iii) adverbial relations (subordinative). For the moment we shall be concerned with the first two categories only.

Co-ordination in medieval narrative poetry generally serves 'to infuse a certain vigour and raciness into the style by cutting out the exact expression of some thought-element to be filled in by the imagination of the audience' (Ohlander 1936, p. 10). Co-ordinate clauses in series are a characteristic feature of the description of rapid and often violent actions:

Amis 2071. To þe lazer he stirt in the wain / & hent him in his honden tvain / & sleynt him in þe lake, / & layd on, as he were wode, / & al þat euer about him stode / Gret diol gan make

Orfeo A 91. In þe orchard to þe quene hye come, / & her vp in her armes nome, / & brouȝt hir to bed atte last, / & held hir þere fine fast

BD 395. I wolde have kaught hyt, and anoon / Hyt fledde, and was fro me goon; / And I hym folwed, and hyt forth wente / Doun by a floury grene wente / Ful thikke of gras, ful softe and swete

NPT 3375. This sely wydwe and eek hir doghtres two / Herden thise hennes crie and maken wo, / And out at dores stirten they anon, / And syen the fox toward the grove gon, / And bar upon his bak the cok away, / And cryden, 'Out! harrow! and weylaway! / Ha! ha! the fox!' and after hym they ran, / And eek with staves many another man

MancT 303. And to the crowe he stirte, and that anon, / And pulled his white fetheres everychon, / And made hym blak, and refte hym al his song, / And eek his speche, and out at dores hym slong / Unto the devel, which I hym bitake

The syntax of such passages serves an obvious mimetic function in giving prominence to the verbal action in a sequence of short co-ordinate clauses. In *BD* 395–9 there is the further suggestion of a breathless narrator, whose impulsiveness at this moment of excitement is expressed not only by his use of co-ordination, but also by the sudden shift from *hyt* to *hym* in referring to the puppy that leads him toward the Man in Black.

While co-ordination is to be found throughout Chaucer's poetry, it is a marked feature of the fabliau in particular, where it 'helps to create the impression of a world full of violent yet disorganized activity, and one where action is more important than explanation or understanding' (Spearing 1979, pp. 64–5). This observation is made with the climax of *The Reeve's Tale* in mind.

Cp the Lambeck comment.

125

This John stirte up as faste as ever he myghte,
And graspeth by the walles to and fro,
To fynde a staf; and she stirte up also,
And knew the estres bet than dide this John,
And by the wal a staf she foond anon,
And saugh a litel shymeryng of a light,
For at an hole in shoon the moone bright;
And by that light she saugh hem bothe two,
But sikerly she nyste who was who,
But as she saugh a whit thyng in hir ye.
And whan she gan this white thyng espye,   4302
She wende the clerk hadde wered a volupeer,
And with the staf she drow ay neer and neer,
And wende han hit this Aleyn at the fulle,   4305
And smoot the millere on the pyled skulle,   4306
That doun he gooth, and cride, 'Harrow! I dye!'
Thise clerkes beete hym weel and lete hym lye;
And greythen hem, and tooke hir hors anon,
And eek hire mele, and on hir wey they gon.
And at the mille yet the tooke hir cake
Of half a busshel flour, ful wel ybake.   (4292-312)

The use of co-ordination in this stretch of fast-paced narrative is so
considerable as to include the presentation of related thoughts and
actions in a linear sequence. Where we might expect subordination, we
find simple juxtaposition instead: the wife jumped up *and* knew the
interior better than John did *and* found a stick by the wall (4294-6); she
drew closer with the stick *and* thought to hit Aleyn *and* hit the miller
(4304-6). As the Spearings observe with regard to the second instance,
'in his courtly style, Chaucer would not have made line [4305] a separate
statement, but would have been more likely to write something like,
"Wening han hit . . ."' (Spearing 1979, p. 64). Even the reversal of
expectation at the very climax of the action ('*And* smoot the millere') is
not formally signalled. It would be natural to expect the adversative
conjunction *but* at this point; but events have by now taken on a life of
their own well beyond the control of the hapless wife, who appropriately
disappears from the narrative without even having an opportunity to
register surprise. Co-ordination is thus used not simply to enact the
speed of events, but also to portray a world of mere sequence in which
the only logic is the logic of the moment. One of the very few instances
of subordination in this passage, rather than expressing a logical mode
of thought, shows the wife jumping to an unfortunate conclusion:

And whan she gan this white thyng espye,
She wende the clerk hadde wered a volupeer,
And with the staf she drew ay neer and neer.   (4302-4)

The wife could be more easily forgiven for her mistake if, believing that
the student wore a night-cap, she saw something white and struck at it,
but this belief is in fact presented as a deduction made on the spur of the

Why illogical? Surely she has to see the thing before she draws a conclusion

moment. The illogical inversion of clauses in lines 4302–3 aptly expresses an impulsive pattern of thought and behaviour that precludes sympathy and heightens the comedy.

Co-ordination is also a feature of summaries, where its function is not to convey an impression of speed, but to draw together related events in a compact and unified statement. As the Man of Law observes, employing co-ordination to condense his material, 'The fruyt of every tale is for to seye: / They ete, and drynke, and daunce, and synge, and pleye': *706, 7*

This comes in gratuitously as I remember it; prolix rather condensed.

> *Havelok* 2930. But sone nam until his lond, / And seysed it al in his hond, / And liuede þer-inne, he and his wif, / An hundred winter in god lif, / And gaten mani children samen, / An liueden ay in blisse and gamen

> *LGW* 2144. And Theseus is lad unto his deth, / And forth unto this Mynotaur he geth, / And by the techyng of this Adryane / He overcom this beste, and was his bane; / And out he cometh by the clewe agayn / Ful prively, whan he this beste hath slayn; / And by the gayler geten hath a barge, / And of his wyves tresor gan it charge, / And tok his wif, and ek hire sister fre, / And ek the gayler, and with hem alle thre / Is stole awey out of the lond by nyghte, / And to the contre of Ennopye hym dyghte / There as he hadde a frend of his knowynge

> *MkT* 2354. And with his legione he took his weye / Toward Cenobie, and, shortly for to seye, / He made hire flee, and atte laste hire hente, / And fettred hire, and eek hire children tweye, / And wan the land, and hom to Rome he wente

This form of sentence-construction is especially favoured as a device of *abbreviatio* in *The Legend of Good Women*; in *The Monk's Tale* it helps to suggest a 'characteristic tone of flat truth' similar to that which P. J. C. Field (p. 38) finds in the chronicle style of Malory. It is a general feature of Chaucer's use of co-ordinate clauses in an extended series that, as in *LGW* 2144–56 above and *RvT* 4292–312 quoted earlier, they tend to become shorter as the passage progresses and to culminate in a somewhat more expansive construction.

Other effects may be achieved by means of co-ordination. In the following lines Medea's love for Jason is presented as a necessary consequence of his noble bearing and reputation:

> Now was Jason a semely man withalle,
> And lyk a lord, and hadde a gret renoun,
> And of his lok as real as a leoun,
> And goodly of his speche, and familer,
> And coude of love al the art and craft pleyner
> Withoute bok, with everych observaunce.
> And, as Fortune hire oughte a foul myschaunce,
> She wex enamoured upon this man. (*LGW* 1603–10)

The suggestion of necessity here ('*and* she fell in love with him') is a more characteristic feature of co-ordination in homiletic romances like *The Man of Law's Tale*, where the simple sentence-structure accords with the heroine's submission to authority:

> Therwith she looked bakward to the londe,
> And seyde, 'Farewel, housbonde routhelees!'
> And up she rist, and walketh doun the stronde
> Toward the ship,—hir folweth al the prees,—
> And evere she preyeth hire child to holde his pees;
> And taketh hir leve, and with an hooly entente
> She blisseth hire, and into ship she wente.   (862–8)

Life is merely sequential in the legend as in the fabliau, though for a different reason, of course. The use of co-ordination in this passage suggests, moreover, something of the heroine's dignified reticence and composure at a time of trial, her emotions being kept in check by the relentlessly serial structure of the sentence. A rather different use of co-ordination, to convey a pretence of strong emotion, is to be seen in the following lines:

> And with the word he gan to waxen red,
> And in his speche a litel wight he quok,
> And caste asyde a little wight his hed,
> And stynte a while; and afterward he wok,
> And sobreliche on hire he threw his lok,
> And seyde, 'I am, al be it yow no joie,
> As gentil man as any wight in Troie.'   (*Tr* V.925–31)

The simple sentence-structure of this stanza serves to draw attention to the contrived appearance of embarrassment and humility with which the wily Diomede, a copy-book lover, hopes to reinforce his argument, and it is all the more effective in coming as a sudden contrast to the involved syntax of his speech to Criseyde in the preceding lines. Against this background of short co-ordinate clauses the repeated phrase 'a litel wight' stands out with particular force; and there is a further suggestion of affected sensibility in the delicately inexplicit treatment of Diomede's swoon ('and afterward he wok'), which, given the onward movement of the sentence, must have been a rather brief one. The phrase 'and afterward' perhaps contains just a hint of the humorously compressed time-scale of romance in *The Miller's Tale*:

> This Nicholas gan mercy for to crye,
> And spak so faire, and profred him so faste,
> That she hir love hym graunted *atte laste*.   (3288–90)

It remains to mention Chaucer's use of *and* in the adversative relation. Although Ohlander (1936, pp. 11–42) distinguishes several varieties of this use in ME. texts, the following examples are confined to constructions in which the conjunction is equivalent to 'but' or 'and yet':

Havelok 1279. But Hauelok sone anon she kiste, / *And* he slep, and
nouht ne wiste / Hwat þat aungel hauede seyd

Orfeo A 389. Of folk þat were þider y-brouȝt, / & þouȝt dede, &
nare nouȝt

Gamelyn 337. He wold they had lenger abide and they seyde nay

BD 395. I wolde have kaught hyt, and anoon / Hyt fledde

LGW 2186. And gropeth in the bed, *and* fond ryght nought

KnT 2449. Men may the olde atrenne, and nought atrede

The continuative force of *and* gives point to the expression of a fact that
is contrary to expectation, since the contrast is not immediately apparent. The construction may thus be used to express surprise and to
enliven a paradox. As we have seen, it comes with special force in the
rush of *and*s at the climax of *The Reeve's Tale* (line 4306).

Asyndetic Co-ordination

Chaucer uses various forms of asyndetic co-ordination in his poetry. *And*
is sometimes left unexpressed in a series of single words, this being a
simple figure of diction called *articulus* by medieval rhetoricians. The
figure differs from normal English usage in the omission of *and* before
the last item in a series:

Anel 169. She wepith, waileth, swowneth pitously

Tr III.1718. He spendeth, jousteth, maketh festeynges

LGW 1166. She waketh, walweth, maketh many a breyd

KnT 1221. He wepeth, wayleth, crieth pitously

FranklT 819. She moorneth, waketh, wayleth, fasteth, pleyneth

In all but one of these lines the asyndetic co-ordination of verbs occurs
with reference to the activities of an unfortunate lover; and it is interesting to observe other common features, such as the alliterative pairing of
verbs beginning with *w*, which testify to a consistent relationship between language and situation. *Tr* III.1718, on the other hand, describes
Troilus at a time of happiness. In either case the use of asyndeton is
perhaps not so much to call attention to the nature of each action in the
series as to suggest an emphatic generalisation of the lover's condition.
The asyndetic co-ordination of object-nouns is found in related contexts
in Chaucer's love poetry:

LGW 1273. and songes wolde he make, / Justen, and don of armes
many thynges, / Sende hire lettres, tokens, broches, rynges

FranklT 947. Of swich matere made he many layes, / Songes, com-
pleintes, roundels, virelayes

The refusal to link the items formally is appropriate to the description of
hopeful activity in the first example and of frustration in the second; in

both, asyndeton effectively suggests an indiscriminate, 'shot-gun' attempt to achieve success. By contrast, the asyndetic co-ordination of subject-nouns does not seem to occur with emotive effect:

Orfeo A 415. Her crounes, her cloþes schine so briȝt
LGW 2613. The flour, the lef is rent up by the rote
Thop 730. His heer, his berd was lyk saffroun

The suspensive nature of this construction possibly deterred ME. writers from exploiting its rhetorical potential. It is infrequent in Chaucer's poetry, and may have been used in *Sir Thopas* in imitation of the style of the rhyming romances.

The asyndetic co-ordination of principal clauses is fairly common in some ME. poetry. Here first are examples in which the clauses normally keep the same subject and verb:

Havelok 939. He bar þe turues, he bar þe star, / þe wode fro the
   brigge he bar
Havelok 1229. þou shalt ben louerd, þou shalt ben syre, / And we
   sholen seruen þe and hire
Havelok 1902. He broken armes, he broken knes, / He broken
   shankes, he broken thes

Such usage is typical of the vigorous vernacular rhetoric based on repetition that is to be found in this romance. The form and rhythm of the first two examples, in which a couplet containing three clauses assigns two to the first line and one to the second, survived in ballads, but is not represented in Chaucer's octosyllabic verse. The simplest type of clausal asyndeton in his poetry occurs in such lines as *Anel* 293 'I wepe, I wake, I faste', where of course only the subject is repeated; beyond this the clauses tend to take on the character of separate sentences, for they lack the brevity, repetition, and emphatic rhythm that weld them together in the examples from *Havelok*.

In another form of asyndeton the subject changes throughout a series of clauses:

Launfal 341. þe cloþ was spred, þe bord was sette; / þey wente to
   hare sopere
Emaré 832. They drowgh up sayl and leyd out ore; / The wynde
   stode as her lust wore, / The wethur was lyth on le
CA V.3752. The dai was clier, the Sonne hot, / The Gregeis were in
   gret doute
LGW 2610. The torches brenne, and the laumpes bryghte; / The
   sacryfices ben ful redy dighte; / Th'ences out of the fyre reketh
   sote; / The flour, the lef is rent up by the rote
SqT 293. The usshers and the squiers been ygoon, / The spices and
   the wyn is come anoon, / They ete and drynke

Sentences of this kind are characteristically found in descriptive writing, where they often serve a preparatory function, with something of an anticipatory effect. The 'ballad construction' to be seen in *Launfal* 341 and *CA* V.3752, where three clauses are fitted into two lines of verse, was later revived by Scott and Coleridge, and its use on several occasions by Gower suggests a more particular indebtedness than Chaucer's to the native tradition of rhyming poetry.

This is the place to mention headless co-ordinate clauses, in which either *and* or a subject-pronoun is omitted:

Orfeo A 319. To a leuedi he was y-come, / ʌ Biheld, & haþ wele vnder-nome

BD 194. And dyde as he hade bede hym doon; / ʌ Took up the dreynte body sone

Tr IV.1218. And he bigan to glade hire as he myghte; / ʌ Took hire in armes two, and kiste hire ofte

Tr V.729. Ful rewfully she loked upon Troie, / ʌ Biheld the toures heigh and ek the halles

Headless constructions can be traced back to OE., where, according to S. O. Andrew (pp. 72ff.), they belong specifically to poetic usage: *Beowulf* 7 'he þæs frofre gebad, / weox under wolcnum, weorðmyndum þah'. A distinctive feature of such clauses is that they expand or re-formulate the content of the clause preceding them; and in this they differ from the asyndetic co-ordinate clauses commonly found in ME. rhyming romances and alliterative poetry, which convey additional rather than more specific information:

Gowther 553. Thei leype on hors, toke schyld and speyr

GGK 2080. Mist muged on þe mor, malt on þe mountez

The asyndetic co-ordination of subordinate clauses also occurs in Chaucer's poetry, though only a few points of his usage will be touched on here. Contiguous relative clauses, when they stand in the same grammatical relation to the antecedent and are both either restrictive or non-restrictive, may be in asyndetic co-ordination:

Amis 1571. As man þat þenkeþ his liif to long, / þat liueþ in treye & tene

BD 129. Throgh Juno, that had herd hir bone, / That made hir to slepe sone

HF 529. This egle, of which I have yow told, / That shon with fethres as of gold, / Which that so hye gan to sore

A desire for emphasis would seem to account for the occasional expression of a second relative pronoun in place of *and*. Similarly emphatic is the asyndetic co-ordination of concessive clauses:

131

Tr II.484. And here I make a protestacioun, / That in this proces if ye depper go, / That certeynly, for no salvacioun / Of yow, though that ye sterven bothe two, / Though al the world on o day be my fo, / Ne shal I nevere of hym han other routhe

and of conditional clauses:

BD 261. this shal he have, / Yf I wiste where were hys cave, / Yf he kan make me slepe sone

BD 968. For every wight of hir manere / Myght cacche ynogh, yif that he wolde, / Yif he had eyen hir to beholde

GenProl 143. She was so charitable and so pitous / She wolde wepe, if that she saugh a mous / Kaught in a trappe, if it were deed or bledde

Such sentences can suggest a process of refinement in setting out the conditions. The last example neatly sums up the Prioress's sensibility by limiting the expression of an already trivial sense of pity to occasions which, in keeping with her affectation of courtly manners, arouse a delicately feminine response to the sight of blood. Pity the poor mouse who suffers less spectacularly!

II PARATAXIS

The word Parataxis may be used in two senses; it may mean simply a lack of grammatical subordination such as we find in the language of children and some primitive peoples, or, secondly, it may be a rhetorical device by which a subordinate relation is idiomatically expressed by a co-ordinately juxtaposed sentence, as when we say 'Knock and it shall be opened' instead of 'If ye knock, it shall be opened'. (Andrew, p. 87)

Here we shall be concerned with parataxis in the second sense, and attention will also be given to some forms of asyndetic parataxis. With respect to clauses connected by *and*, it may be noted that although Ohlander (1936) arranges his comprehensive survey of co-ordination in ME. according to the logical relationships that obtain between the clauses, very few of the constructions are paratactic. The following sentence is quoted as an example of the temporal relation: *Arthour* A 1311 'þe messangers herden þis / And wonder hadde þerof ywis'. But the relationship between these clauses is not grammatically subordinative; nor, logically, is the temporal relation the only one that might be assigned to the construction. Purely logical distinctions should not be pressed too far, since ultimately they question the existence of a norm in the use of *and* as a clausal conjunction. To quote Kellner once again, 'it is scarcely possible to connect sentences together without a certain kind of *hypotaxis* or subordination' (p. 52).

In sentences like 'Knock and it shall be opened', 'Give him an inch and he'll take a mile', the imperative is equivalent to a subordinate clause of condition, and the construction is therefore known as the conditional imperative. It occurs in OE. (see *OED* s.v. *and* conj. 8b) and is extremely common from the ME. period onwards. Ohlander (1936, pp. 52–72) has a full discussion of the varieties of this construction in ME., and Eitle (pp. 157–8) provides a brief description of Chaucer's usage. Here are some examples:

> *Havelok* 922. Go þu yunder, and sit þore, / And y shal yeue þe ful
>   fair bred
> *Amis* 298. Broþer, be now trewe to me, / & y schal ben as trewe to
>   þe
> *Tr* III.1106. Seye 'al foryeve', and stynt is al this fare
> *Tr* IV.466. Thynk nat on smert, and thow shalt fele non
> *WBT* 1096. What is my gilt? For Goddes love, tel me it, / And it
>   shal been amended, if I may
> *SqT* 328. Trille this pyn, and he wol vanysshe anoon
> *SecNT* 502. I rede thee, lat thyn hand upon it falle, / And taste it
>   wel, and stoon thou shalt it fynde

The conditional force is weakest when there is an element of verbal parallelism, as in *Amis* 298–9 and such expressions as 'You scratch my back and I'll scratch yours'. In the examples quoted above, in which a particular person is addressed, the reference is to a specific occasion. The construction has also a more general application in proverbial statements and the like, where it is used as what Jespersen (p. 315) calls the 'imaginary imperative':

> *LGW* 735. As, wry the glede, and hotter is the fyr; / Forbede a love,
>   and it is ten so wod
> *WBProl* 519. Forbede us thyng, and that desiren we; / Presse on us
>   faste, and thanne wol we fle
> *PardProl* 354. If cow, or calf, or sheep, or oxe swelle / That any
>   worm hath ete, or worm ystonge, / Taak water of that welle and
>   wassh his tonge, / And it is hool anon

There are two other forms of the paratactic expression of condition with a co-ordinating conjunction in Chaucer's poetry. In the first of these, the introductory clause equivalent to the protasis in a conditional sentence is interrogative rather than imperative (see Ohlander 1936, pp. 62–6):

> *Fox&Wolf* 186. Woltou nou mi srift ihere, / And al mi liif I shal þe
>   telle?
> *Tr* III.883. Quod the Criseyde, 'Wol ye don o thyng, / And ye
>   therwith shal stynte al his disese?'

133

MLT 341. But lordes, wol ye maken assurance, / As I shal seyn, assentynge to my loore, / And I shal make us sauf for everemore?

Modern punctuation necessarily tends to obscure the fact that this interesting construction joins a statement to a question in a dependent relationship. Such sentences have the reduced force of polite requests, avoiding on the one hand the abruptness of the conditional imperative itself, and on the other hand the remoteness of the supposition in paratactic constructions employing a verb in the subjunctive mood. The other form of expression to be mentioned here, with the alternative co-ordinating conjunction *or*, is more familiar:

Havelok 1772. Vndo swiþe, and lat us in, / Or þu art ded, bi seint Austin

Octavian 1163. For youre mete moste ye paye, / Or ye gete tham no more

Tr I.953. Now loke that atempre be thi bridel, / And for the best ay suffre to the tyde, / Or elles al oure labour is on ydel

Tr IV.924. So lef this sorwe, or platly he wol deye

MkT 2161. To which ymage bothe yong and oold / Comanded he to loute, and have in drede, / Or in a fourneys, ful of flambes rede, / He shal be brent that wolde noght obeye

NPT 3006. Now help me, deere brother, or I dye

Lastly, the concessive relation might also be expressed paratactically in ME. (see Ohlander 1936, pp. 22–9). In interrogative constructions of the following kind, *and* is equivalent to 'although' or 'even though':

HSynne 539. 'Why,' seyd he, 'wyl hyt nat ryse, / And y haue do þe same wyse?'

Ipomadon 1154. Foole, will þou lyghtly goo / Fro thy love, and lovys her soo?

KnT 2835. 'Why woldestow be deed,' thise womman crye, / 'And haddest gold ynough, and Emelye?'

NPT 2920. Have ye no mannes herte, and han a berd?

CYProl 636. Why is thy lord so sluttish, I the preye, / And is of power bettre clooth to beye?

A feature of this usage is the ellipsis of a subject-pronoun in the second clause when, as is usually the case, the clauses have a common subject. The construction is also found in statements:

Octavian 646. To lerne hys crafte forto do, / And hys kynde was nevyr therto

Gamelyn 148. For to loken if thou were strong and art so ying

SqT 200. Hou that it koude gon, and was of bras

In the interrogative form especially this construction has a pointedness that is appropriate to the expression of bewilderment or surprise. The formal equivalence of the clauses sharpens the logical contrast, and the ellipsis in the second clause is conducive to brevity.

Asyndetic Parataxis

Three forms of asyndetic parataxis are to be found in Chaucer's poetry. First, there are constructions in which a subordinating conjunction has been omitted, leaving two formally independent clauses in juxtaposition: *MerchT* 1391 'They been so knyt ʌ ther may noon harm bityde'. Elliptical sentences of this kind will not be dealt with here. Secondly, there are constructions in which subordination is indicated by the front-shifting of a verb in the subjunctive mood: *WBProl* 336 'Have thou ynogh, thee thar nat pleyne thee'. Finally, there are various constructions in which a subordinative relation is not formally marked, but is implied by their strong logical coherence and, in the spoken language, by such features as juncture and intonation. Although no single quotation can usefully stand to represent this category, an example would be if the clauses in the line from *The Merchant's Tale* quoted above were inverted to give 'Ther may noon harm bityde, they been so knyt'. Some of the constructions to be considered here may be compared with those in which *and* is expressed, but the majority have no syndetic equivalents.

There are two ways of expressing the conditional relation by means of asyndetic parataxis in Chaucer's poetry. The first of these is simply the asyndetic form of the conditional imperative. Chaucer appears to use this construction mainly in its function as an 'imaginary imperative' introduced by the verbs *let* and *take*:

Arthour A 1272. Comeþ þider þer ich ȝou lede, / Mi moder ȝe schullen se

Havelok 911. But yeveþ me inow to ete, / Fir and water y wile yow fete

HF 737. loo, thou maist alday se / That any thing that hevy be, / As stoon, or led, or thyng of wighte, / And bere hyt never so hye on highte, / Lat goo thyn hand, hit falleth doun

WBT 1139. Taak fyr, and ber it in the derkeste hous / Bitwix this and the mount of Kaukasous, / And lat men shette the dores and go thenne, / Yet wole the fyr as faire lye and brenne / As twenty thousand men myghte it biholde

MancT 163. Taak any bryd, and put it in a cage, / And do al thyn entente and thy corage / To fostre it tendrely with mete and drynke / Of alle deyntees that thou kanst bithynke, / And keep it al so clenly as thou may, / Although his cage of gold be never so gay, / Yet hath this brid, by twenty thousand foold, / Levere in a forest, that is rude and coold, / Goon ete wormes and swich wrecchednesse

MancT 177. And lat hym seen a mous go by the wal, / Anon he weyveth milk and flessh and al

These are not paratactic

The last two examples but one illustrate the considerable lengths for which the construction could be sustained, and the concomitant re-inforcement of the apodosis by the conjunctive adverb *yet*. In *MancT* 163–71, moreover, 'Yet hath this brid . . .' serves as a principal clause to both the conditional imperative and the concessive clause 'Although his cage of gold be never so gay', which is itself a blend of hypotactic and paratactic forms of construction.

Bad grammar

The second and more common method of expressing the conditional relation is by the front-shifting of a subjunctive verb in the protasis:

Havelok 1782. Shol ich casten þe dore open, / Summe of you shal ich drepen

Gowther 521. Had eydur of hom byn to lacke, / Full evyll we had ben al devoured

PF 610. Ye, have the glotoun fild inow his paunche, / Thanne ar we wel

Tr I.530. For, be myn hidde sorwe iblowen on brede, / I shal byjaped ben a thousand tyme

Tr IV.583. but hadde ich it so hoote, / And thyn estat, she sholde go with me

WBProl 329. Have thou ynogh, what thar thee recche or care / How myrily that othere folkes fare?

WBT 1008. Koude ye me wisse, I wolde wel quite youre hire

CYT 846. And konne he letterure, or konne he noon, / As in effect, he shal fynde it al oon

The construction does not commonly occur in OE. texts, but it is amply represented in ME. (see Visser, pp. 900–1). It has various connotations according to form and context, ranging from the expression of possibility with verbs in the present subjunctive to pure hypothesis with verbs in the preterite subjunctive; in constructions with the present subjunctive of *have* it has the force of a clause introduced by 'so long as'. The 'imaginary imperative' is also found in this form:

Tr II.483. But cesse cause, ay cesseth maladie

Tr II.1387. And reed that boweth down for every blast, / Ful lightly, cesse wynd, it wol aryse

The concessive relation is often similarly expressed by means of a front-shifted verb in the subjunctive mood, as in 'Be it ever so humble, there's no place like home', though it is not necessary for the concessive clause to precede the principal clause. This construction is common in Early English (see Visser, pp. 907–9), where it differs from MnE. usage in its somewhat wider range of forms and applications, and in its use of *never* rather than *ever* for adverbial reinforcement:

Havelok 1114. Ne noman bringen hire to bedde, / But he were king, or kinges eyr, / Were he neuere man so fayr

Tr II.1034. Were his nayles poynted nevere so sharpe, / It sholde maken every wight to dulle

Tr II.1203. Now, goode nece, be it nevere so lite, / Yif me the labour it to sowe and plite

Tr V.1289. 'How myghte I than don,' quod Troilus, 'To knowe of this, yee, were it nevere so lite?'

WBT 943. For, be we never so vicious withinne, / We wol been holden wise and clene of synne

CYT 1016. That she wolde suffre hym no thyng for to paye / For bord ne clothyng, wente he never so gaye

Chaucer also uses the paratactic form of alternative concession, where the contrastive pairs consist of predicate nouns or adjectives (see Visser, pp. 909–10):

HF 2072. Were the tydynge soth or fals, / Yit wolde he telle hyt natheles

PF 503. And I wol seye my verdit fayre and swythe / For water-foul, whoso be wroth or blythe

KnT 1839. This is to seyn, she may nat now han bothe, / Al be ye never so jalouse ne so wrothe

WBT 1157. He nys nat gentil, be he duc or erl

Finally, a special form of paratactic concession found in Chaucer's poetry may be represented by the expression 'be as be may', where the verb is repeated and the impersonal subject is not expressed (compare 'be that as it may'):

Tr V.796. Happe how happe may, / Al sholde I dye, I wol hire seche

LGW 1852. 'Be as be may,' quod she, 'of forgyvyng, / I wol not have noo forgyft for nothing'

MkT 2129. Be as be may, I wol hire noght accusen

A very common form of parataxis in ME. is what may be called the inverted consecutive construction, as in 'Everyone liked him, he was so friendly'. Here the order of clauses in the equivalent hypotactic and elliptical sentences ('He was so friendly (that) everyone liked him') is inverted. The first clause may be referred to as the principal clause, and the second, containing the adverb *so*, as the intensive clause. The effect of this order is to place the intensive clause in an emphatic position, though in some contexts its importance is reduced to the expression merely of attendant circumstance. Three varieties of the inverted consecutive construction may be distinguished according to the structure of the intensive clause. Here first are some examples in which this clause, whose verb is usually the copula *be*, has its subject and predicate in normal order:

Havelok 840. I wene that we deye mone / For hunger, þis dere is so strong

ABC 11. Thou canst not warne him that with good entente / Axeth thin helpe, thin herte is ay so free

LGW 2669. And he shal slepe as longe as evere thee leste, / The narcotyks and opies ben so stronge

SqT 419. That ther nys tygre, ne noon so crueel beest, / That dwelleth outher in wode or in forest, / That nolde han wept, if that he wepe koude, / For sorwe of hire, she shrighte alwey so loude

PardT 865. Ye, sterve he shal, and that in lasse while / Than thou wolt goon a paas nat but a mile, / This poysoun is so strong and violent

CYT 751. we semen wonder wise, / Oure termes been so clergial and so queynte

The construction is also found when an adverb or predicate adjective preceded by *so* is front-shifted in the intensive clause:

Amis 814. þe douke strok after swiche a dent / þat þurch þe dore þat fauchon went, / So egre he was þat tide

HF 867. and shewe hym swyche skiles / That he may shake hem be the biles, / So palpable they shulden be

HF 962. And gladded me ay more and more, / So feythfully to me spak he

Tr IV.228. Lith Troilus, byraft of ech welfare, / Ibounden in the blake bark of care, / Disposed wood out of his wit to breyde, / So sore hym sat the chaungynge of Criseyde

MillT 3611. Lo, which a greet thyng is affeccioun! / Men may dyen of ymaginacioun, / So depe may impressioun be take

SqT 507. It was so wrapped under humble cheere, / And under hewe of trouthe in swich manere, / Under plesance, and under bisy peyne, / That no wight koude han wend he koude feyne, / So depe in greyn he dyed his coloures

In the third form of the construction the verb of the intensive clause follows *so* in front position. Thus beside 'it was so bright' and 'so bright it was' we find in ME. the now unfamiliar inversion 'so was it bright':

Havelok 2146. þat men se mouhte, by þe liht, / A peni chesen, so was it briht

PP B V.199. She sholde nouȝte haue walked on that welche, so was it thredebare

Anel 56. That everych other slough, so were they wrothe

Tr V.36. For ire he quook, so gan his herte gnawe

KnT 2692. As blak he ~~(ay)~~ as any cole or crowe, / So was the blood
   yronnen in his face

PhysT 126. Anon his herte chaunged and his mood, / So was he
   caught with beautee of this mayde

MkT 2644. no thing myghte aswage / Hys hye entente in armes and
   labour, / So was he ful of leonyn corage

It will be noticed that the inverted consecutive construction, in all its
forms, is a mainly descriptive device. The choice of forms is determined
by practical considerations and the kind of emphasis required, the
second type in particular lending special prominence to adjectives and
adverbs.

Some of the examples that have been given illustrate a symmetrical
arrangement whereby a consecutive sentence is followed by an intensive
clause for a further measure of emphasis. Normal and inverted consecutive constructions are also found side by side or in other forms of
combination:

BD 1015. Therwith she loved so wel ryght, / She wrong do wolde to
   no wyght. / No wyght myghte do hir noo shame, / She loved so
   wel hir owne name

MerchT 1774. He was so ravysshed on his lady May / That for the
   verray peyne he was ny wood. / Almoost he swelte and
   swowned ther he stood, / So soore hath Venus hurt hym with
   hire brond

Thop 778. Sire Thopas eek so wery was / For prikyng on the softe
   gras, / So fiers was his corage, / That doun he leyde him in that
   plas

In the first two examples a consecutive sentence is followed by the
inverted form so as to effect a rhetorical chiasmus; and it will be noticed
that with the ellipsis of the consecutive conjunction in *BD* 1016 the
passage has the appearance of four separate statements. In the last
example the intensive clause 'So fiers was his corage' is embedded in a
consecutive sentence, the position of the clause helping to emphasise its
absurd inappropriateness in this context.

There is, in conclusion, an interesting construction that occurs so
often in similar contexts in ME. narrative poetry as to be little more than
an intensive tag:

Octavian 1645. He bad hys modur make hur yare / Into Fraunce
   wyth hym to fare: / He wolde no lenger byde

Launfal 457. Of Karlyoun þe ryche constable / Rod to Launfal,
   wythout fable: / He nolde no lengere abyde

MerchT 1805. ~~(his)~~ hastif Januarie / Wolde go to bedde, he wolde no
   lenger tarye

The construction consists in the contrastive relationship between a clause containing a verb of motion and a clause normally containing the auxiliary *wolde*, a negative adjunct, and a verb of rest such as *abide*, *dwell*, or *tarry*. The second clause generally has the meaning 'without further delay', and the construction as a whole often suggests an inverted expression of sentences like the following:

> *Arthour* L 81. þeo kyng wolde no lengur byde / Bot dyȝt him to schip þat tyde
>
> *Amis* 2305. No lenger stint he no stode, / Bot hent his kniif wiþ dreri mode
>
> *Tr* II.598. Criseyde aros, no lenger she ne stente, / But streght into hire closet wente anon

The origin of the construction, however, would appear to lie in the paratactic expression of the final relation in OE. by means of a headless clause introduced by *wolde* (see Andrew, pp. 87–8). In *Beowulf* 1338 'ond nu oþer cwom / mihtig man-scaða, wolde hyre mæg wrecan', for example, the second clause is equivalent to a participial clause of purpose ('wishing to avenge her kinsman'). The original sense of the ME. construction, which differs from OE. usage in the expression of a subject-pronoun and in the exclusively negative form of the clause, may therefore have been 'not wishing to delay any further'.

In another form of this construction there is a more emphatic order of words, with the adjunct in front position:

> *Amis* 2435. Wel he þouȝt to quyte hur mede, / No lenger wold he abyde
>
> *Octavian* 1445. He sprange as fowle dothe yn flyght, / No lenger wolde he byde
>
> *SumT* 1736. He wente his wey, no lenger wolde he reste
>
> *PardT* 851. And forth he goeth, no lenger wolde he tarie
>
> *ShipT* 250. And doun he goeth, no lenger wolde he lette
>
> *NPT* 3034. And forth he gooth—no lenger wolde he lette— / Unto the west gate of the toun
>
> *KQuair* 74. And vp I rase, no langer wald I lye

Sentences of this kind are less often found with adjuncts like 'for nothing' and 'for no man' in Chaucer's poetry:

> *Amis* 1046. & lepe astite upon his stede, / For noþing he nold abide
>
> *LGW* 1187. Love wol love, for nothing wol it wonde

Because they have the same metrical value, 'for nothing' and 'no longer' are interchangeable in those contexts where the difference in meaning is immaterial. This form of the stereotyped expression may be compared with a hypotactic equivalent:

Amis 550. & þouȝt sche wold for noman wond / þat sche ne wold to him fond

Amis 1610. Anon sche dede men timber take, / For noþing wold sche wond

The complex sentence in the first example contains a negative clause in the consecutive relation. The same information might have been conveyed as in the second sentence by means of parataxis: '& þouȝt sche wold to him fond, / For noman wold sche wond'.

It is appropriate to conclude with this construction. For one thing, W. Weese (p. 181) plausibly suggests that Chaucer's use of it is an instance of his indebtedness to the idiom of the rhyming romances; and one of the aims of the present study has been to provide further evidence of Chaucer's relation to the native poetic tradition. Moreover, the construction itself exhibits a feature of ME. syntax that has a special significance for the study of style in medieval poetry. Like many of the other constructions we have considered, it is particularly adapted to the purpose of emphatic expression, and thus contributes to the intensive note of much medieval narrative, by virtue of its negative form. Perhaps in no other period of English has negation been such an important factor of literary style.

Bibliography

The place of publication is London, unless otherwise noted.

TEXTS

Alisaunder	*Kyng Alisaunder*, edited by G. V. Smithers, EETS 227, 237, 2 vols (1952–7)
Amadace	*Sir Amadace*, in *Six Middle English Romances*, edited by Maldwyn Mills (1973)
Amis	*Amis and Amiloun*, edited by MacEdward Leach, EETS 203 (1937)
Arthour	*Of Arthour and of Merlin*, edited by O. Macrae-Gibson, EETS 268, 279, 2 vols (1973–9)
Athelston	edited by A. McI. Trounce, EETS 224 (1951)
Beowulf	edited by C. L. Wrenn, revised by W. F. Bolton (1973)
CA	*Confessio Amantis*, in *The English Works of John Gower*, edited by G. C. Macaulay, EETS ES 81–2, 2 vols (1900–1)
Caxton, *Charles*	*Lyf of Charles the Grete*, edited by S. J. Herrtage, EETS 36–7, 2 vols (1880–1)
CMundi	*Cursor Mundi*, edited by Richard Morris, EETS 57, 59, 62, 66, 68, 99, 6 vols (1874–93)
Emaré	in *Six Middle English Romances*, edited by Maldwyn Mills (1973)
Fox&Wolf	*The Fox and the Wolf*, in *Early Middle English Verse and Prose*, edited by J. A. W. Bennett and G. V. Smithers, second edition (Oxford, 1968)
Gamelyn	*The Tale of Gamelyn*, edited by W. W. Skeat, second edition (Oxford, 1893)
GGK	*Sir Gawain and the Green Knight*, edited by J. R. R. Tolkien and E. V. Gordon, second edition revised by Norman Davis (Oxford, 1967)
Gowther	*Sir Gowther*, in *Six Middle English Romances*, edited by Maldwyn Mills (1973)

Guy I	*The Romance of Guy of Warwick*, edited by Julius Zupitza, EETS ES 42, 49, 59, 3 vols (1883–91)
Guy II	*The Romance of Guy of Warwick: The Second or 15th-Century Version*, edited by Julius Zupitza, EETS ES 25–6, 2 vols (1875–6)
HarlLyr	*The Harley Lyrics*, edited by G. L. Brook, fourth edition (Manchester, 1968)
Havelok	*The Lay of Havelok the Dane*, edited by W. W. Skeat, revised by Kenneth Sisam (Oxford, 1915)
HSynne	*Robert of Brunne's Handlyng Synne*, edited by F. J. Furnivall, EETS 119, 123, 2 vols (1901–3)
Ipomadon	edited by E. Kölbing (Breslau, 1899)
Isumbras	*Sir Isumbras*, in *Six Middle English Romances*, edited by Maldwyn Mills (1973)
KQuair	James I of Scotland, *The Kingis Quair*, edited by John Norton-Smith (Oxford, 1971)
LybDes	*Lybeaus Desconus*, edited by M. Mills, EETS 261 (1969)
Maldon	*The Battle of Maldon*, edited by E. V. Gordon (1937)
Malory	*Works*, edited by Eugène Vinaver, second edition (Oxford, 1971)
MandTravels	*Mandeville's Travels*, edited by M. C. Seymour (Oxford, 1967)
Melayne	*The Sege of Melayne*, in *Six Middle English Romances*, edited by Maldwyn Mills (1973)
Octavian	in *Six Middle English Romances*, edited by Maldwyn Mills (1973)
Orfeo	*Sir Orfeo*, edited by A. J. Bliss, second edition (Oxford, 1966)
ParlAges	*The Parlement of the Thre Ages*, edited by M. Y. Offord, EETS 246 (1959)
Patience	edited by J. J. Anderson (Manchester, 1969)
Peace	*In Praise of Peace*, in *The English Works of John Gower*, edited by G. C. Macaulay, EETS ES 81–2, 2 vols (1900–1)
PP	Langland, *The Vision of William Concerning Piers the Plowman*, edited by W. W. Skeat, 2 vols (Oxford, 1886)
Purity	*Cleanness*, edited by J. J. Anderson (Manchester, 1977)
RelLyr XIV	*Religious Lyrics of the XIVth Century*, edited by Carleton Brown, second edition revised by G. V. Smithers (Oxford, 1957)
Shearmen	*The Shearmen and Taylors' Pageant*, in *Two Coventry Corpus Christi Plays*, edited by Hardin Craig, EETS ES 87 (1902)
WedGawen	*The Weddynge of Sir Gawen and Dame Ragnell*, edited by Laura Sumner, Smith College Studies

| | in Modern Languages, Vol. 5, no. 4 (North-ampton, Mass., 1924) |
| *Wynnere* | *A Good Short Debate between Winner and Waster*, edited by Sir Israel Gollancz (1921) |

STUDIES

This list provides a key to references in the present book, and is not intended as a representative selection of writings on the topics that have been dealt with.

Abbott, E. A.,	*A Shakespearian Grammar* (1884)
Andrew, S. O.,	*Syntax and Style in Old English* (Cambridge, 1940)
Auerbach, Erich,	*Mimesis: The Representation of Reality in Western Literature*, translated by Willard R. Trask (Princeton, 1953)
Baum, Paull F.,	*Chaucer's Verse* (Durham, N.C., 1961)
Bennett, J. A. W., ed.,	*Chaucer: The Knight's Tale*, second edition (1958)
Bennett, J. A. W. and G. V. Smithers, eds,	*Early Middle English Verse and Prose*, second edition (Oxford, 1968)
Blake, Norman,	*The English Language in Medieval Literature* (1977)
Brewer, D. S.,	'The Relationship of Chaucer to the English and European Traditions', in *Chaucer and Chaucerians: Critical Studies in Middle English Literature*, edited by D. S. Brewer (1966), pp. 1–38
Bronson, Bertrand H.,	'Chaucer's Art in Relation to his Audience', in *Five Studies in Literature*, University of California Publications in English, Vol. 8, no. 1 (Berkeley, 1940), pp. 1–53
Burrow, J. A., ed.,	*Geoffrey Chaucer: A Critical Anthology* (Harmondsworth, 1969)
———,	*Ricardian Poetry: Chaucer, Gower, Langland and the 'Gawain' Poet* (1971)
Clemen, Wolfgang,	*Chaucer's Early Poetry*, translated by C. A. M. Sym (1963)
Courmont, André,	*Studies on Lydgate's Syntax in 'The Temple of Glas'* (Paris, 1912)
Davie, Donald,	*Articulate Energy: An Inquiry into the Syntax of English Poetry* (1955)
Davis, Norman, ed.,	*Sir Gawain and the Green Knight*, edited by J. R. R. Tolkien and E. V. Gordon, second edition revised by Norman Davis (Oxford, 1967)
Eitle, Hermann,	*Die Satzverknüpfung bei Chaucer* (Heidelberg, 1914)
Elliott, Ralph W. V.,	*Chaucer's English* (1974)
Field, P. J. C.,	*Romance and Chronicle: A Study of Malory's Prose Style* (1971)

144

Firth, J. R.,	'A New Approach to Grammar', in *Selected Papers of J. R. Firth*, edited by F. R. Palmer (1968), pp. 114–25
Foulet, Lucien,	*Petite syntaxe de l'ancien français*, third edition (Paris, 1930)
Geoffrey of Vinsauf,	*Poetria Nova of Geoffrey of Vinsauf*, translated by Margaret F. Nims (Toronto, 1967)
Jambeck, Thomas J.,	'Characterization and Syntax in the *Miller's Tale*', *Journal of Narrative Technique* (1975), 73–85
Jespersen, Otto,	*The Philosophy of Grammar* (1924)
Jonson, Ben,	*The English Grammar*, in *Ben Jonson*, edited by C. H. Herford and Percy and Evelyn Simpson, vol. 8 (Oxford, 1947), pp. 463–553
Karpf, Fritz,	*Studien zur Syntax in den Werken Geoffrey Chaucers* (Vienna and Leipzig, 1930)
Kellner, Leon,	*Historical Outlines of English Syntax* (1892)
Kenyon, J. S.,	*The Syntax of the Infinitive in Chaucer* (1909)
Kerkhof, J.,	*Studies in the Language of Geoffrey Chaucer* (Leiden, 1966)
Lewis, C. S.,	*The Allegory of Love: A Study in Medieval Tradition* (Oxford, 1936)
Macaulay, G. C., ed.,	*The English Words of John Gower*, EETS ES 81–2, 2 vols (1900–1)
MacLeish, Andrew,	*The Middle English Subject-Verb Cluster* (The Hague, 1969)
Masui, Michio,	*The Structure of Chaucer's Rime Words: An Exploration into the Poetic Language of Chaucer* (Tokyo, 1964)
Mustanoja, Tauno F.,	*A Middle English Syntax*, Part I, *Parts of Speech* (Helsinki, 1960)
Novelli, Cornelius,	'The Demonstrative Adjective *This*: Chaucer's Use of a Colloquial Narrative Device', *Medieval Studies* xx (1957), 246–9
Ohlander, Urban,	*Studies on Coordinate Expressions in Middle English* (Lund, 1936)
	'Omission of the Object in English', *Studia Neophilologica* xvi (1943), 105–27
Onions, C. T.,	*Modern English Syntax*, new edition of *An Advanced English Syntax* prepared from the author's materials by B. D. H. Miller (1971)
Palsgrave, John,	*Lesclarcissement de la langue françoyse*, edited by F. Genin (Paris, 1852)
Phillipps, K. C.,	'Asyndetic Relative Clauses in Late Middle English', *English Studies* xlvi (1965), 323–9
Quirk, Randolph and Sidney Greenbaum,	*A University Grammar of English* (1973)
Roberts, W. F. S.,	'Ellipsis of the Subject-Pronoun in Middle English', *London Mediaeval Studies* i (1937), 107–15

Robinson, F. N., ed.,	*The Works of Geoffrey Chaucer*, second edition (Cambridge, Mass., 1957)
Rodway, Allan,	'By Algebra to Augustanism', in *Essays on Style and Language*, edited by Roger Fowler (1966), pp. 53–67
Schlauch, Margaret,	'Chaucer's Colloquial English: Its Structural Traits', *PMLA* lxvii (1952), 1103–16
Sisam, Kenneth, ed.,	*The Nun's Priest's Tale* (Oxford, 1927)
Skeat, W. W., ed.,	*The Complete Works of Geoffrey Chaucer*, 6 vols (Oxford, 1894)
Smith, C. Alphonso,	'The Short Circuit in English Syntax', *Modern Language Notes* xix (1904), 113–21
Spearing, A. C., ed.,	*The Knight's Tale* (Cambridge, 1966)
——,	*The 'Gawain'-Poet* (Cambridge, 1970)
——,	*Criticism and Medieval Poetry*, second edition (1972)
——,	*Chaucer: Troilus and Criseyde* (1976)
Spearing, A. C. and J. E., eds,	*The Reeve's Prologue and Tale with the Cook's Prologue and the fragment of his Tale* (Cambridge, 1979)
Sweet, Henry,	*A New English Grammar: Logical and Historical*, Part II, *Syntax* (Oxford, 1898)
Trounce, A. McI.,	'Chaucer's Imperative with *As*', *Medium AEvum* ii (1933), 68–70
Visser, F. Th.,	*An Historical Syntax of the English Language*, 4 vols (Leiden, 1963–73). The pagination is continuous: Part I (pp. 1–658), Part II (pp. 659–1306), Part III, First Half (pp. 1307–1858), Part III, Second Half (pp. 1859–2470)
Weese, W.,	'Word-Order as a Factor of Style in Chaucer's Poetry' (unpublished Ph.D. dissertation, Yale University, 1950)
Wilson, Louis Round,	'Chaucer's Relative Constructions', *Studies in Philology* i (1906), 1–60

General Index

Abbott, E. A., 53
ambiguity, 89–91
anacoluthon, 1, 72, 74, 76–7
and, adversative conjunction, 128–9;
    co-ordinating conjunction, 124–9;
    introductory particle, 53–7
Andrew, S. O., 131, 132, 140
Anelida and Arcite, 21, 130
Anglo-Saxon Chronicle, 124
anticipation, 80–1
apo koinou, 110, 112, 113, 114, 118
apposition, *see* tag order
articulus, 129
as, expletive, 50–2
asyndetic co-ordination, 31, 129–32
asyndetic parataxis, 135–41
Auerbach, Erich, 8, 108

'ballad construction', 130–1
Baum, Paull F., 35
Beaumont, Sir Francis, 9
Bennett, J. A. W., 90
Bennett, J. A. W. and G. V. Smithers, 21
Bible, 124
binomial verbs, 57–9
Blake, Norman, 5–7, 124
Book of Courtesy, 8
Book of the Duchess, The, 5, 54, 89, 118–19
Brewer, D. S., 9
broken order, 22–33, 102; of adjuncts, 27; of attributive adjectives, 29–33; of complements, 27–8; of objects, 24–5; of subjects, 22–4; of verbs, 25–7; with genitive phrases, 28–9

Bronson, Bertrand H., 8
Brook, G. L., 42, 110
Burns, Robert, 96
Burrow, J. A., 35, 38, 104

Canon's Yeoman's tale, The, 90–1
Canterbury Tales, The, 5
Chestre, Thomas, 38
chiasmus, *see* cross order
Clemen, Wolfgang, 119
close repetition of object, 73–5; of subject, 66–70
Coleridge, S. T., 131
colloquial usage, 2–5
Complaint to his Lady, A, 75
Complaint unto Pity, The, 75
concrete noun clause, 7–8, 81–2
conditional imperative, 133, 135–6
co-ordination, 124–32
Courmont, André, 62
Cowper, William, 106
cross order, 43–6

Dante, 35, 38
Davie, Donald, 4, 105–6
Davis, Norman, 91
discontinuity, 33–43
discontinuous modification, 33–40, 103–6
discontinuous phrasal verb, 37–8
displacement, 19–21
distant repetition of object, 75; of subject, 70–1
double discontinuity, 23, 27, 34, 38
double ellipsis, 89–91, 95

Index of Chaucer Quotations